AQA Danc

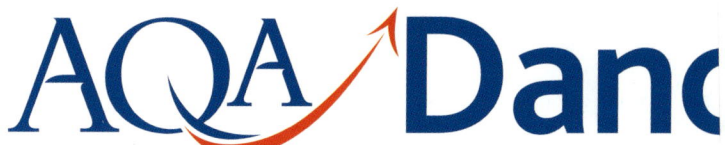

GCSE

Maggie Clunie

Liz Dale

Lyn Paine

Series editor

Lyn Paine

Nelson Thornes

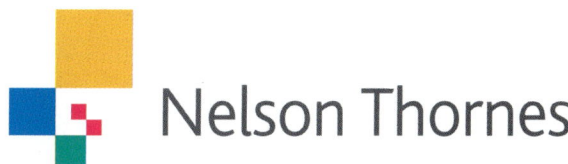

Text © Maggie Clunie, Liz Dale and Lyn Paine
Original illustrations © Nelson Thornes Ltd 2009

The right of Maggie Clunie, Liz Dale and Lyn Paine to be identified as the authors of this work has been asserted by them in accordance with the Copyright, Designs and Patents Act 1988.

All rights reserved. No part of this publication may be reproduced or transmitted in any form or by any means, electronic or mechanical, including photocopy, recording or any information storage and retrieval system, without permission in writing from the publisher or under licence from the Copyright Licensing Agency Limited, of Saffron House, 6–10 Kirby Street, London EC1N 8TS

Any person who commits any unauthorised act in relation to this publication may be liable to criminal prosecution and civil claims for damages.

Published in 2009 by:
Nelson Thornes Ltd
Delta Place
27 Bath Road
CHELTENHAM
GL53 7TH
United Kingdom

09 10 11 12 13 / 10 9 8 7 6 5 4 3 2 1

A catalogue record for this book is available from the British Library

ISBN 978 1 4085 0419 2

Cover photograph by fotopic.net
Illustrations by Angela Knowles
Page make-up by Fakenham Photosetting Ltd
With thanks to Indexing Specialists (UK) Ltd

Printed and bound in Spain by GraphyCems

Contents

Introduction 4

1 Introducing GCSE Dance 5
1.1 What can I expect on the GCSE Dance course? 6
Chapter 1 summary 8

2 Dance styles 9
2.1 Dance in Britain today 10
2.2 The dance style 12
2.3 The choreographer's style 14
2.4 What's your style? 18
Chapter 2 summary 20

3 Safe dance practice 21
3.1 Nutrition and hydration for a dancer 22
3.2 Warm-up and cool-down 24
3.3 Safe practice as a performer ... 26
3.4 Rehearsing safely – what should you wear? 28
3.5 Rehearsing safely – what is in a space? 30
Chapter 3 summary 32

4 The ingredients of dance 33
4.1 Actions 34
4.2 Space 36
4.3 Dynamics 38
4.4 Relationships 40
Chapter 4 summary 42

5 Creating dances 43
5.1 Choosing a stimulus 44
5.2 How to use a stimulus 46
5.3 Motif and development 48
5.4 Choosing a choreographic approach 50
5.5 Choreographic devices 52
5.6 Dance relationships 54
5.7 Group design 58
5.8 Structuring dances 60
5.9 The choreographic process 62
5.10 Choosing and using music 64
5.11 The choreography tasks 66
Chapter 5 summary 68

6 Performing dances 69
6.1 Technical skills in performing .. 70
6.2 Expressive skill in performance 72
6.3 Achieving high-quality performance 74
6.4 Performance in a duo/group dance – Unit 3 76
6.5 Solo set dance – Unit 2 78
Chapter 6 summary 80

7 Aspects of production 81
7.1 Physical setting 82
7.2 The use of features in physical settings 86
7.3 The performing space 88
7.4 The aural setting 90
7.5 Features of accompaniment 92
7.6 The relationships between music and dance 94
7.7 Features of costume 96
7.8 Dance for the camera 98
7.9 Other people involved in dance performance 100
7.10 A comparison of dance works .. 102
Chapter 7 summary 104

8 Preparing for assessment 105
8.1 The written exam 106
8.2 Preparing to be videoed for the set dance 110
8.3 Preparing for the performance and choreography assessment 112
Chapter 8 summary 114

9 Professional works fact file 115
9.1 *Bird Song* and *Faultline* 116
9.2 *Ghost Dances* and *Nutcracker!* 118
9.3 *Overdrive* and *Perfect* 120
9.4 *Romeo and Juliet* and *Rosas Danst Rosas* 122
9.5 *'Still Life' at the Penguin Café* and *Swansong* 124
9.6 Other useful resources 126

Glossary 127

Index 130

Nelson Thornes and AQA

Nelson Thornes has worked in partnership with AQA to ensure this book and the accompanying online resources offer you the best support for your GCSE course.

All resources have been approved by senior AQA examiners so you can feel assured that they closely match the specification for this subject and provide you with everything you need to prepare successfully for your exams.

These print and online resources together **unlock blended learning**; this means that the links between the assessment questions in the book and the revision activities online blend together to maximise your understanding of a topic and help you achieve your potential.

These online resources are available on *kerboodle!* which can be accessed via the internet at www.kerboodle.com/live, anytime, anywhere. If your school or college subscribes to *kerboodle!* you will be provided with your own personal login details. Once logged in, access your course and locate the required activity.

For more information and help on how to use *kerboodle!* visit www.kerboodle.com

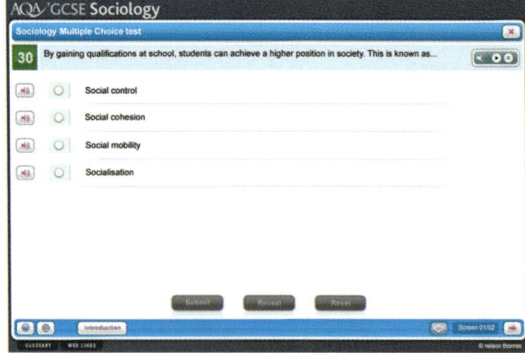

How to use this book

Objectives

Look for the list of **Learning Objectives** based on the requirements of this course so you can ensure you are covering everything you need to know for the exam.

AQA Examiner's tip

Don't forget to read the **AQA Examiner's Tips** throughout the book.

Visit www.nelsonthornes.com/aqagcse for more information. The Controlled Assessment tasks in this book are designed to help you prepare for the tasks your teacher will give you. The tasks in this book are not designed to test you formally and you cannot use them as your own Controlled Assessment task for AQA. Your teacher will not be able to give you as much help with your tasks for AQA as we have given with the tasks in this book.

1 Introducing GCSE Dance

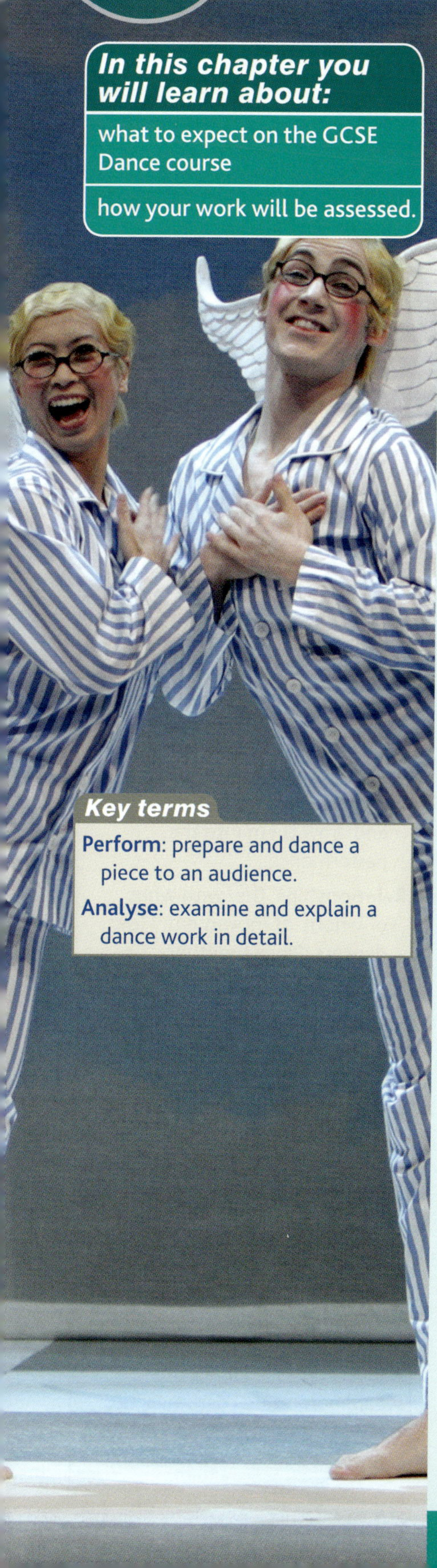

In this chapter you will learn about:
- what to expect on the GCSE Dance course
- how your work will be assessed.

Key terms
- **Perform**: prepare and dance a piece to an audience.
- **Analyse**: examine and explain a dance work in detail.

■ Why choose dance?

In the film *Billy Elliot*, Billy is auditioning for the Royal Ballet School. He is asked at the interview what it feels like when he is dancing and he replies, 'I start stiff and that … it sort of feels good, once I get going I forget everything and disappear … I feel a change in my whole body, flying like a bird, like electricity … yeah, like electricity.'

■ Performer, choreographer, critic and director

Do you, like Billy Elliot, feel good when you dance? Do you like creating dances for yourself and others as well as performing in them? Do you like watching other people dance? If you answered yes to these questions, then GCSE Dance could be the course for you.

In the GCSE Dance course you will learn to **perform**, choreograph, direct and **analyse** dance. As a performer, you will develop confidence and self-esteem, as well as sensitivity to others and team working skills. As a choreographer, you will use the skills of creativity and problem solving to come up with some imaginative ideas for dances. As a critic, you will be able to make informed decisions about the dances you see. In directing others, you will develop your communication skills and your ability to create good working relationships with others. And, by opting for GCSE Dance, you will be taking part in a physical activity that promotes fitness and well being. You will find that by studying dance you will improve your creative skills as well as your physical skills – that is what makes dance unique!

The controlled assessment tasks in this book are designed to help you prepare for the tasks your teacher will give you. The tasks in this book are not designed to test you formally and you cannot use them as your own controlled assessment tasks for AQA.

A *GCSE Dance students in performance*

1.1 What can I expect on the GCSE Dance course?

The skills you will develop

During the GCSE Dance course you will develop your performance, **choreography** and appreciation skills.

Performing dance

You will learn to perform solo and group dances created by yourself and others. You will learn about and develop skills in the following areas.

The technical aspects of performing

- Moving safely, caring for your body and preparing for dance (safety).
- Dancing safely, correctly and accurately within a dance style (technique).
- Being strong enough to perform challenging movements (strength).
- Being able to dance without tiring (stamina).
- Standing and holding yourself correctly (**posture** and **alignment**).
- Stretching to increase your movement range (**flexibility**).
- Rehearsing.
- Using space, **rhythm** and dynamics.
- Working with other dancers.
- Working with music/accompaniment.
- Working with props.

The expressive aspects of performing

The expressive aspects of performing are important because they draw an audience into a dance and help the audience to understand the meaning or the idea of the dance. Expressive aspects of dance include:

- **Focus** and eye-line: where a dancer looks when performing. For example, whether they look out to the audience or at another dancer. If a group of dancers are performing in unison, it is important that their eye-line is the same, and this gives a polished finish to a dance.
- **Projection**: communicating emotion and the meaning or intention of the dance to an audience through, for example, exaggerating movements and extending them through the limbs and torso, facial expression, and the energy and power of the performance.
- Extension of the body and limbs: where a dancer uses their body to make very clear shapes, stretching the body, arms, legs and feet in order to make each movement as clear to an audience as possible.
- Communicating with other dancers: where dancers use their focus and projection to help the audience understand **relationships** between the dancers and within the performance.

Choreographing dance

Choreography means 'making' dance. During the GCSE Dance course you will choreograph solo and group dances. This will involve:

> **Objectives**
>
> Learn about the performance, choreography and appreciation skills you will develop throughout the course.

> **Key terms**
>
> **Choreography**: the art of creating dance.
> **Posture**: body position.
> **Alignment**: the correct placement of body parts in relation to other body parts.
> **Flexibility**: the range of movement that is attainable in a joint or muscle.
> **Rhythm**: repeated patterns of movements or sounds.
> **Focus**: using the eyes to enhance performance or interpretative qualities.
> **Projection**: when a dancer gives out appropriate energy to connect with an audience and draw them into the performance.
> **Relationships**: the 'with what or whom' of movement. How dancers dance together.

> **Did you know ??????**
>
> Focus is important because it helps the audience to understand the meaning of the work as they watch the dancer.

> **AQA Examiner's tip**
>
> You will be assessed on safety during all practical assessments, so make sure that you and your dancers remove all jewellery, wear appropriate costumes, tie hair back if necessary and are not chewing gum!

- developing a vocabulary of the ingredients of dance – actions, space, dynamics and relationships
- using your own and others' ideas (including those of professional choreographers) to make dance
- finding and using different starting points to make dances, for example a painting or a poem
- exploring ideas through movement
- selecting and developing movements
- structuring and shaping dances.

A 'Still Life' at the Penguin Café *is choreographed by David Bintley*

> **Key terms**
>
> **Appreciate:** show knowledge and understanding of your own and others' dances and of dance in general.
>
> **Describe:** write or talk about what something looks or sounds like or is made up of.
>
> **Interpret:** understand and explain the meaning of a dance through action, costume, set design/lighting and accompaniment.
>
> **Evaluate:** to consider the value, quality or importance of something.

Appreciating dance

You will study a range of dances in different styles to develop your appreciation skills and to understand more about performance and choreography. You will learn to use dance terminology to **appreciate**, **describe**, **interpret**, analyse and **evaluate** the movement content, set design, lighting, costume, accompaniment and features of dance for the camera. You will also reflect on and evaluate your own and other students' performance and choreography.

> **Activity**
>
> 1. Look at Photo **A** which is taken from *'Still Life' at the Penguin Café*.
>   a Describe the costume the penguin is wearing.
>   b Give two ways in which the mask the dancer is wearing helps our understanding of the dance work.
>   c Explain one advantage and one disadvantage of wearing a mask when performing.

Assessment

The GCSE Dance course is designed to take two years and it has four units. It will be possible to complete some units, such as the performance of the set solo dance, in the first year of study. Table **B** shows how Units 1, 2, 3 and 4 are assessed. You can see that Units 1 and 2 will be assessed by an examiner who is not your teacher. Units 3 and 4 will be marked by your teacher and moderated by an AQA moderator. You will need to prepare a short programme note to support your choreography of a solo or group dance in Unit 4. This should include the title of your dance, the name and artist of your chosen music/accompaniment and a brief outline of your dance idea.

Marked by an examiner	Marked by your teacher
Unit 1	Unit 4
Critical Application	**Choreography**
Written examination	Controlled assessment
20%	40%
	15% for the solo composition task
	25% for the choreography of a solo/group dance
Unit 2	Unit 3
Performance of a set Dance	**Performance in a Duo/Group Dance**
Practical examination	Controlled assessment
20%	20%

B How GCSE Dance is assessed

Chapter summary

In this chapter you have learnt:

From this chapter you should have gained a good understanding of what to expect during your GCSE Dance course. You will have discovered that there is a strong focus on performing, choreographing and appreciating your own, other students' and professional dance works. Throughout this book you will be given lots of tips from AQA examiners to help you succeed in all areas.

During the GCSE course you might learn about choreography in an 8–10-week unit, using ideas such as paintings, poetry, sculpture or a story from the newspapers to create motifs, develop your understanding of using choreographic devices, understand how to structure choreography and help you or your dancers to improve their skills when performing.

Activity

1. Look at Photo **A**. It shows the cupids in Matthew Bourne's *Nutcracker!*
   a Describe the costumes worn by the dancers.
   b Why do you think the dancers are dressed identically?
   c What do the wings represent?

A *Nutcracker!* is choreographed to Tchaikovsky's music score

In order to achieve in dance, you must:

✔ know your strengths and how to improve your weaknesses
✔ have a desire to improve
✔ be open to new ideas and new styles of dance
✔ be creative
✔ enjoy dancing and watching dance
✔ be able to work alone and with others
✔ be able to give and receive feedback
✔ be able to analyse dance.

2 Dance styles

In this chapter you will learn about:
- why people dance
- the wide range of dance styles in Britain today
- stylistic features of dances
- your own individual style.

Key terms

Style: characteristic features of a dance work or choreographer's work that enable it to be recognised as belonging to that particular group.

Technique: a specific way of moving according to particular rules and conventions.

Isolation: moving a part of the body independently, such as a shoulder shrug.

Accompaniment: the sound that you hear during the dance, for example percussion.

Contemporary: a group of dance styles originating in the early 20th century created by individuals working outside the Classical ballet style, in response to the conditions of modern life.

Starter activity

- Write down all of the different styles and types of dance that you can think of.
- Sort them into groups. You could use these headings: social/recreational dance, traditional dance, and dance for an audience (theatrical).
- Find a way to present this information, for example, a mind map, spider diagram or a venn diagram.

Ways of dancing

During this course you will learn to perform in different styles. You will also learn about the different styles used by choreographers and dance companies. In this chapter you will think about dance 'flavours' – what makes dances different from, and similar to, each other.

Everyone dances. All over the world people dance for different reasons. Dance is a way of understanding yourself, the groups and communities that you live in and the world around you. Dance is a powerful way of expressing and communicating feelings and experiences that cannot be expressed in words and there are many ways of doing this. Think of all these 'ways' of dancing as **styles**. This GCSE course focuses on performing, choreographing and appreciating dances that are artistic and that are made for an audience.

Different uses of the word 'style'

In GCSE Dance we use the word 'style' in several ways. First, we often use it to describe a particular **technique** that has specific movement content or vocabulary. For instance, a technique class in jazz style would include **isolations** of different body parts such as shoulders and ribcage, limb and torso stretches and rhythmic movement patterns.

We also use the word 'style' to describe the choreography: the way in which the movement material is presented, selected and organised; the way in which the idea or theme is treated; and aspects of production such as **accompaniment**, lighting, costume and set. Styles and techniques are always changing and developing because choreographers are influenced by the time and world in which they live.

Each 'family' of styles such as **contemporary** dance, ballet, jazz, African and South Asian dance includes different styles that share common features but that have developed differently. For instance, the jazz family could include musical theatre, tap and some street dance styles. Dance styles are continually evolving and barriers are breaking down so that new mixes are created such as physical theatre which crosses the boundaries of theatre and dance.

2.1 Dance in Britain today

Activity

1. Look at Photos **A** to **E** of people dancing in Britain today.
   a. What is the purpose of each dance? Is it social/recreational dance, traditional dance or dance for an audience?
   b. Describe the features of each dance.

   An example for Photo **A** has been completed for you.

Objectives

Consider the reasons why people dance.

Be aware of the wide range of dance styles in Britain today.

Key terms

Formations: shapes or patterns created by a group of dancers.

Who? Six men.

What? A traditional dance (you can tell by the costumes, head-dresses and footwear). The performers will have learned this dance. It could be quite old and passed from generation to generation.

When? Probably in the spring or summer, in recent times (use the environment or setting as a clue).

Why? Possibly to mark a festival or a special occasion.

A Morris dancers performing in England

How? They are using steps and **formations**, and they are holding sticks.

Where? On a road in an urban environment.

Chapter 2　Dance styles　11

B　*This dancer is performing a piece called* Into the Hoods

C　*People of all ages can dance*

D　*The* Afrika Afrika *show. This company boasts more than 100 artists, dancers, singers and musicians*

E　*Young dancers performing on stage*

Activity

2　Using the photographs:
a　find two dances that are similar and discuss what they have in common
b　find two dances that are different and discuss what makes them so different.

2.2 The dance style

Dance language

In order to dance well together, dancers need to learn the same dance 'language'. This usually involves training the body in a specific technique and learning a vocabulary of movements that contain the features of the style. Some styles have developed their own distinctive vocabulary with names for specific **actions**. Think of the French terms used in ballet, such as *plié*, *jeté* and *arabesque*.

Many dance styles will have particular ways of using the body, actions, **dynamics** and **space**. Here are some physical features with an example of a dance style for each:

- Stance: how the body is held, for example the relaxed stance, bent knees and low centre of gravity typical of African dance.
- Use of body parts: for example, isolation of the shoulders and ribs in jazz dance.
- Use of centre and spine: for example, **contraction** and **extension** in some contemporary dance styles.
- Body design: typical shapes and positions, for example, angular body shapes in street dance.
- **Gestures**: for example, the intricate hand gestures of South Asian dance.
- Travelling: ways of stepping and jumping across the floor, for example long, low runs in jazz dance.
- Initiation: how and where movements are initiated or started, for example, the use of breath and the centre of the torso to initiate the action in contemporary dance.
- Dynamic qualities: the speed, flow and energy of the movements, for example, the smooth, sustained bending and stretching actions in ballet.
- Rhythmic qualities: emphasis and timing, for example, how different body parts and actions produce **syncopated** rhythms in street dance.
- Floor-work: moving towards, on and away from the floor, for example the use of the floor for spins, rolls and balances in street dance.

Applying features to different styles

Table **A** shows how features can be applied to different styles: South Asian style (**Bharata Natyam**) and a contemporary style (**Graham based**) are used as examples. Choose another dance style and write the features of that style in the space provided in the table.

> **Objectives**
>
> Recognise the features of specific dance styles.
>
> Understand how technique and style relate.

> **⊙⊙ links**
>
> You might like to refer to the Glossary on page 127 and also to Chapter 5, Creating dances.

> **Key terms**
>
> **Actions**: what a dancer does, for example leap, spin, balance.
>
> **Dynamics**: the 'how' or 'quality' of movement.
>
> **Space**: the 'where' of movement.
>
> **Contraction**: shortening of a muscle or muscles.
>
> **Extension**: lengthening one or more muscles or limbs.
>
> **Gestures**: actions or movements of a body part which is not weight bearing.
>
> **Syncopated**: stressing a beat that is not normally stressed.
>
> **Bharata Natyam**: a classical South Asian dance style, characterised by intricate hand gestures and fast footwork.
>
> **Graham based**: a contemporary dance style created by Martha Graham in the 1930s. Characterised by angular body shapes and use of breath and the centre of the body to initiate movements.
>
> **Contact**: when dancers touch, lean, lift or support each other.

> **Activity**
>
> 1. Choose a specific dance style. Imagine you are taking part in a technique class in this style. What would you expect to be included?

A Features of different dance styles

Feature	Bharata Natyam	Graham based	Style 3
Stance	Upright and erect	Body aligned, neutral	
Use of body parts	Flexed feet, precise hands Eyes follow hands Facial expressions important	Feet parallel and turned out Hands are natural	
Use of centre and spine	Upright and straight	Contracts, extends, tips and tilts	
Body design	Quite angular, symmetric and asymmetric	Angular and curved shapes	
Gestures	Expressive hands and face	Abstract patterns made by arms and legs	
Travelling	Dancers skim across the floor, heels often lead	Large range of steps and step patterns, including walks and runs	
Initiation	Hands often lead	Movements initiated by breath and centre of spine	
Use of weight and energy	Contained	Used to suspend, swing, drop, etc.	
Dynamic qualities	Precise, contrasts in speed and flow	Full range used, energy important	
Rhythmic qualities	Important – feet often set the rhythms	Found in the movements themselves	
Floor-work	Unusual in classical style, medium level mainly used	Floor used as much as other levels	

B The intricate hand gestures associated with Bharata Natyam draw an audience into the dance

Activities

2. Using the vocabulary of an English country dance (travelling, turning, meeting, parting and **contact**) create a short, simple, group dance for 4–5 dancers.

3. Choose a specific style in which to perform the dance.

4. Find an appropriate piece of music to accompany your dance.

5. Show your dance to others – do they recognise the style?

6. What did you have to emphasise to express the style?

2.3 The choreographer's style

A choreographer's style will be influenced by a number of factors including:

- The dance technique they trained in.
- The people they have danced with and danced for.
- The dancers they choreograph for.
- Their interest in other art forms.
- What interests and inspires them.
- The time and place that they inhabit.

Objectives

Identify the distinctive features of different dances.

Know that some choreographers use ideas from different cultures.

links

Find out more in Chapter 5, Creating dances and Chapter 7, Aspects of production.

Case study

Siobhan Davies

Siobhan Davies was initially interested in art and she studied sculpture. She attended classes at the London Contemporary Dance School and then performed with the London Contemporary Dance Theatre. She trained and worked with Richard Alston. Siobhan visited America twice, training in Cunningham technique the first time and in alternative techniques the second time. Her partner, David Buckland, is an artist and photographer and she often choreographs for more unusual venues such as art galleries.

A Siobhan Davies

Activities

1. Read the case study about Siobhan Davies. How might these life experiences influence her work?
2. Research the background of another choreographer.
3. What life experiences influence their work?

Stylistic features

Apart from the dance technique used by the dancers and the choreographer, and the influences on the choreographer, there are other ways in which the styles of dances differ. These include:

- The movement vocabulary (actions, space, dynamics, relationships).
- The treatment of the theme or subject matter.
- **Choreographic approaches**.
- **Choreographic form** and **choreographic devices**.
- The relationship between the dance and the accompaniment.
- Other aspects of production such as lighting, set and costume.
- The performance environment.
- Combining with other art forms and media such as film.

> **Key terms**
>
> **Choreographic approaches**: how choreographers work with the dance material, for example by using the dancers' improvisations.
>
> **Choreographic form**: giving the dance a shape and structure, for example by using contrasting sections.
>
> **Choreographic devices**: using different methods to repeat, develop and vary the material.
>
> **Narrative**: a dance that tells a story.

Case study: Matthew Bourne

A dance in the style of Matthew Bourne might include the following features:

- Balletic and contemporary style.
- Literal gestures.
- Characterisation.
- Theatrical elements, with colourful, outrageous set and costumes.
- A new spin on a classic ballet or opera story.
- Comedy and **narrative**.
- A large cast.
- Classical music as accompaniment.

Activities

4. Look at section 4 of Christopher Bruce's *Swansong* and Act 1, Scene 1 of Kenneth MacMillan's *Romeo and Juliet*.
5. Compare how the theme of power is explored in each dance through actions, dynamics, space and relationships.

Extension activity

Work with a partner to create a short duo exploring the theme of power. Perform and choreograph your duo in a specific style.

Activities

6. Look at the dance of the little swans or cygnets in Matthew Bourne's *Swan Lake* (Act 2) and compare this with the dance of the little swans in the original classical version by Marius Petipa to see how the choreographers have treated the subject matter.
7. Find at least three similarities and three differences in style.

Influences from different cultures

For many years choreographers have borrowed and combined styles of dance from different cultures to enhance their ideas and create new vocabularies. In *'Still Life' at the Penguin Café*, David Bintley uses ballroom, African, carnival and English folk-dance styles to explore the idea of animals and cultures in danger of extinction all over the world. Christopher Bruce uses tap and jazz dance styles in a sinister way in *Swansong* as the guards interrogate the victim. In *Faultline*, Shobana Jeyasingh uses hand gestures which combine features of Bharata Natyam, contemporary, pedestrian and street dance styles to communicate ideas about identity and youth culture.

Activities

8. Look at the Hog-nosed Skunk Flea dance in *'Still Life' at the Penguin Café*.
9. What does David Bintley add to the morris dance to communicate his ideas?

Choreographers' distinctive styles

B *Richard Alston Dance Company performing* Overdrive

> ❝ I think of myself as a sculptor or a painter ... I love what movement does. I love what the human body tells you ... my sense of movement is like drawing, is like making marks in the space. ❞
>
> Richard Alston, Alston in Overdrive (DVD)

> ❝ My work is about the image that is created in the piece. I'm also fascinated by film and the moving image. Secondly, it's exploring the relationship between these images and the dynamics – that's what will make it [the dance] work for the audiences, and finally, I would say that truth is vitally important. ❞
>
> Kevin Finnan, speaking about Perfect, www.motionhouse.co.uk

C *Motionhouse Dance Theatre performing* Perfect

Chapter 2 Dance styles 17

D 'Still Life' at the Penguin Café, *David Bintley/Birmingham Royal Ballet*

> " It was a deliberate choice that I would have as great a variety of animals as I could find as I wanted the piece to represent all four corners of the world. It was also important to me that a particular dance style could be equated with each animal and that a particular geographical location would also play a part in determining the style of each dance. "
>
> David Bintley, 'Still Life' at the Penguin Café, *GCSE Study Notes*

> " I usually avoid programme notes for my ballets because they tend to limit the audience's imagination … My works generally contain a collage of ideas creating several possible narratives which in turn will hopefully trigger a personal and unique reaction in the spectator. This is true of Swansong, in which an element of surprise also helps build tension. "
>
> Christopher Bruce, Swansong *Study Notes, Rambert Dance Company*

E Swansong, *choreographed by Christopher Bruce*

2.4 What's your style?

Your experience of dance styles

During the course you will experience different dance styles. You will study dances made by different choreographers and performed by different companies. The dances prescribed by AQA have been selected for the range and variety of styles that they represent. You will learn to perform dances in different styles and you may take classes in different techniques. You may have the opportunity to be taught by different dance teachers and visiting dancers. Think about the differences in their style of movement; how they teach; how they choreograph and the ideas and accompaniment that they like to use. You may also attend classes, dance activities and performances out of school that are similar to or different from the dance styles you learn in school.

How styles are assessed in GCSE Dance

The written paper

Your understanding of style will help you to describe, analyse, interpret and evaluate two professional works in the written paper.

The set dance

There is a choice of **two** set solo dances to perform. Each will have its own distinctive features. Make sure you are clear about what these are. The selection of action, space and dynamic content and the way in which these are structured and varied will contribute to the style. The way in which the dance relates to the accompaniment will also reflect the style. Marks will be awarded for your ability to perform in the style and mood of the original choreography.

Performance in a dance

This group piece will be based on one of the professional works you have studied. It must have three clear links with the chosen work. These can include the dance style, the choreographic style, the subject matter, the accompaniment, the action content, characterisation, props, costume, staging or setting. If dance style is not one of the links, the dance must be in a specific style. For example, you could perform a trio based on the characters of the ghosts in *Ghost Dances* by Christopher Bruce. The three links might be:

- The dance style – contemporary.
- Characterisation – the ghosts.
- Accompaniment – South American folk music.

Objectives

Reflect on your experience of dance styles.

Reflect on your own individual style.

links

Find out more in Chapter 5, Creating dances.

AQA Examiner's tip

Make sure you are clear about the links to the professional work selected as a basis for your performance in a dance.

AQA Examiner's tip

Study, know and use the key features of the style of the set dance that you will perform for the exam.

Solo composition task

This task is based on a different professional work to that selected for the performance in a dance, so it is likely to have a different style. You will be able to make decisions about the accompaniment and the style, providing it is appropriate and helps you to meet the criteria for assessment. For example, you could select three **motifs** from the opening section of *Bird Song*. You would then develop these and link them together to form a new dance, which does not have to be in the same style as the original.

Your distinctive style

The dance and choreographic style that you develop will depend upon the following:

- Technical training – learning, improving and extending your physical skills.
- Vocabulary – generating your own movements, improvising and finding new ways of moving and interpreting ideas.
- Choreography – your interests, influences, approach, how you work with other dancers, how you research and collect ideas.

> **Key terms**
>
> **Motifs**: patterns or designs of action content that encapsulate an idea and can be repeated and developed throughout the dance.

> **Activities**
>
> 1. Design costumes, lighting and a set for a dance you have performed or choreographed.
> 2. If you were able to work with a composer, what would the accompaniment be like?
> 3. What is the overall effect you want to achieve?

A *What accompaniment might complement this style of dance?*

Chapter summary

In this chapter you have learnt:

In this chapter you have reflected on why people dance and the different styles of dance in Britain today. You should now have a good understanding of the context for GCSE Dance. You will have knowledge and understanding of the features of style that dances share, and also what makes them different. You should be able to recognise and describe some of these features.

You have looked at the dancer's style and the choreographer's style and this will help your performance, choreography and appreciation skills. Throughout the chapter examples of different professional works have been used and you may wish to find out more about some of those. You may also want to see other dances by the same choreographer. You will appreciate that the course units and assessment tasks require you to perform in and know about different styles, and you will have given some thought to your own performance style and your unique choreographic style.

Activity

What is your style? To help you think about what you need to do to develop your sense of style and achieve original choreographies and effective performances, complete this table of your strengths and areas for development.

A *Strengths and areas for development*

Feature	Strengths	Areas for development
Dance styles or techniques experienced		
Movement vocabulary you like to use (especially range of actions)		
Types of dance you enjoy watching, for example narrative, abstract, comic, dramatic, lyrical		
Types of accompaniment you have used		
Your ideas/stimuli for dances		
Your interest in other art forms		
Choreographers that you know about and admire		

3 Safe dance practice

In this chapter you will learn about:

- nutrition and hydration for a dancer
- warm-up and cool-down
- safe practice as a performer
- rehearsing safely, wearing appropriate clothing and using an appropriate space.

Why safe dance practice is important

Being safe as a dancer is vitally important. Knowing how to prepare your body for activity, how to take care of it when it is moving and how to contribute to a productive and safe working environment is fundamental to your experience as a dancer.

Professional performers take injury very seriously because it could cost them their career, so they pay a great deal of attention to safe dance practice. The same applies to you because you are studying for GCSE Dance. If you injure yourself you might not be able to participate in lessons, which means you would miss vital work – and that might affect your final grade.

What is safe dance practice?

Safe dance practice is all about making sure your body is prepared for the incredible demands you are going to make on it and about ensuring that you know how to work safely with others. It is about understanding how your choice of dance-wear and the space you rehearse or perform in can affect your work and it is about knowing what to do and how to deal with things if they go wrong.

A A dancer preparing to land safely after a jump

3.1 Nutrition and hydration for a dancer

As a dancer you are going to expect a lot from your body, so it is really important to make sure you get proper nourishment (that is, nutrition). If you are going to perform at your best, you will need energy, strong bones, flexible joints and muscles, and lungs that work efficiently. Energy comes from the food you eat, which is turned into fuel for the body. If you put dirty, low-grade fuel in a car you would not be surprised if it broke down, and the same principle applies to your body. A healthy diet is essential if you want your body to work efficiently.

Objectives
- Learn what constitutes a healthy diet for a dancer.
- Learn how to plan your own healthy eating.
- Learn the importance of hydration.

A healthy diet

Source **A** shows the essential ingredients of a healthy diet. The bigger the portion on the plate, the more you should eat from the group. How does this compare with your diet?

Key terms

Nutrition: obtaining the food necessary for health.

Lactic acid: a waste product which builds up in the muscles during exercise.

Hydrated: provided with an adequate amount of water.

Activity

1. Draw up a typical week's healthy eating plan for a dancer who is attending classes, taking part in rehearsals during the day and resting in the evenings.

A The eatwell plate

Chapter 3 Safe dance practice 23

Muscles need energy to work. Energy comes from food which is converted to glucose (sugar). To work efficiently muscles also need plenty of oxygen. Glucose and oxygen are carried to the muscles in the bloodstream, and waste products such as carbon dioxide are taken away in the blood.

Hydration

When we work hard we sweat more, and during this process we lose water and vital body salts as well as heat. We must replace the water and the salts otherwise we get cramp and **lactic acid** builds up. Lactic acid builds up during continuous use of the same muscle groups and after a while it makes the muscles ache and feel heavy. Then it causes cramp and eventually the muscles stop working altogether. If you have ever tried to walk up an escalator or a long flight of stairs and felt the muscles in your legs begin to burn and get heavier, you have experienced the effect of lactic acid build up.

Regular sips of water during a dance session keep the body **hydrated** and the muscles working at optimum level. Obviously when you are dancing you will be working hard and you will sweat more than usual, so you need to consume more than the recommended two litres of fluids per day. If you start to feel thirsty this is a sign that you need to sip water more regularly.

> *Remember*
> Eating a healthy diet is good for you, but it can only be really effective when it forms part of an overall healthy lifestyle.

> *Activity*
> 2   Design a colourful, eye-catching and informative poster suitable for the wall of a studio to advertise healthy eating. Remember the water!

> *Did you know* ??????
> If you feel thirsty, you are already dehydrated.

B *Sip water regularly to stay hydrated*

3.2 Warm-up and cool-down

Why do you need to warm up?

A warm-up in dance is not the same thing as just being warm, so wearing a hoodie and turning up the heating is not an effective warm-up for a dance session! A proper warm-up prepares the body and focuses the mind so that you are ready for more strenuous dance activity. When you eat a piece of toffee, it takes lots of chewing to turn it into a supple, pliable mass. This is exactly what you are trying to achieve with your body during a warm-up, but it is a gradual process and you should never try to over-exert your body or raise your pulse and breathing rates too quickly during a warm-up.

You warm-up for three reasons:

- to reduce the possibility of injury
- to improve performance
- to prepare psychologically.

> **Objectives**
>
> Learn why you need to warm-up and cool-down in dance.
>
> Understand what changes occur in the body during a warm-up and a cool-down.
>
> Discover how to plan your own warm-up and cool-down.

A *Dance students participating in a warm-up session*

What happens in a warm-up?

A good warm-up gradually raises the body temperature and heart rate, resulting in increased blood flow to the muscles. The blood carries oxygen which acts as fuel for the muscles, and the increased flow of blood warms them and makes them more elastic and therefore more efficient and less susceptible to strain and sprain injuries. In addition, nerve messages from the brain to the limbs speed up and joints and ligaments are lubricated.

A warm-up is a gradual process and it cannot be rushed. It can take more than 10 minutes to do an effective warm-up, and it should be done before every dance activity irrespective of whether what follows is a technique class or something less physically demanding. If you break for longer than 15 minutes during a dance activity, you will need to warm up again. By the end of a good warm-up you should feel more alert, better coordinated and full of energy.

The stages of an effective warm-up

Gentle pulse-raising activity
Start with 3–5 minutes of gentle pulse-raising activity to gradually increase internal body temperature. For example:

- slow walking in different directions and to varying tempos
- slow jogging on the spot, changing direction, dodging imaginary obstacles
- short, simple combinations of the above.

Joint mobility
Rhythmical, swinging movements focusing on mobilising the joints in the body. For example:

- whole-body activities (torso bending, curling, stretching)
- movements such as knee bends which involve large muscle groups
- isolations and combinations of circling/reaching of specific body parts, for example arms, shoulders, wrists, hips, feet, etc.
- leg and arm swings.

Flexibility
Stretches which involve the big muscles in the body. These should be dynamic stretches held for no longer than 10 seconds at a time.

Core stability
Exercises which focus on body alignment and the use of the centre of the body for control or core stability.

> **Key terms**
> **Direction**: the pathway of a movement.
> **Dynamic stretches**: slow, controlled movements through the full range of motion.
> **Core stability**: relates to the use of the centre of the body to stabilise the body during movement.

Cool-down

You must never stop strenuous physical activity suddenly. A cool-down at the end of the class is essential to:

- allow the heart rate to gradually return to normal
- prevent the build-up of waste products or toxins such as lactic acid in the muscles, thereby helping to prevent muscle stiffness and soreness
- prevent pooling of blood in the muscles, which can cause you to feel dizzy due to reduced blood supply to the brain.

A cool-down may include slow exercises or passive stretching and could mirror the early part of the warm-up in content. Breathing exercises are also useful. Before starting your cool-down, put on more layers of clothing, so that the process happens gradually.

> **Remember**
> - If recovering from an injury or illness you must consult a doctor before taking part in dance activity.
> - If you feel pain during a warm-up, stop immediately.
> - Take care to perform movements with correct placement and alignment.
> - If you do not warm up properly, there is a much greater risk of injury occurring.

> **Activities**
> 1. Work in pairs to devise your own warm-up and then teach it to the rest of your class.
> 2. Make sure you work both sides of the body equally.
> 3. If you use music, make sure you choose something that has a slow-to-medium tempo and a regular beat.

> **links**
> You can find more information about warming up and cooling down at **www.young-dancers.org** by clicking on the 'body' link.

3.3 Safe practice as a performer

Landing after a jump

Look at Photo **A**, which shows dancers in a leap. They rely on their knees to act as shock absorbers and cushion the impact on landing. As a dancer your knees are your best friends, so remember to use them as well as your feet when you land after any kind of **elevation**.

A Your knees take the strain when you land after a jump

Working with others

When you are working with others you need to concentrate hard and pay close attention at all times. You will need to rely much more on your **peripheral vision** and if you are working well in a group it will almost feel like you have switched on a sixth sense. You will have to work sensitively together and be aware of the shared responsibility for your orientation in the space and in relation to each other. If you do not think about these things when you are working with others the dance will not look as polished and, even worse, you might collide with others and cause injuries.

Supporting and lifting

Safety takes priority in supports and lifts, so never attempt to do something that you feel unhappy about, however easy someone else makes it look. Dancers must have sufficient strength and maturity to carry out lifts with proper placement and alignment. Lifts should always be taught carefully and slowly by a qualified teacher.

Weight sharing

Mutual trust and confidence are essential ingredients when you are working in this way. Talk through what you are trying to achieve before you attempt to do it and never try to surprise your partner by suddenly doing something that you have not discussed first. Be clear about how you will recover from your moves and always maintain control of your own weight. Always work slowly and carefully when you are planning your work because speed can increase the risk of injury.

Objectives
Learn how to perform safely with others.

Learn how to treat minor injuries.

Key terms
Elevation: the action of 'going up' without support, such as in a jump.

Peripheral vision: what you can see happening at the outer edges of your range of vision without actually moving your eyes or your head.

AQA Examiner's tip
An audience likes to see dance moves executed safely. If it looks under-rehearsed or dangerous it will spoil the performance, so do not attempt a move unless you are sure it looks and feels safe!

Chapter 3 Safe dance practice 27

> **Activity**
> Design an eye-catching and informative poster for a dance studio showing how you would treat a sprain or strain injury.

B *Take responsibility for your partner's safety as well as your own when performing a lift*

C *Plan your moves in advance*

> **links**
> To find out more about common dance injuries look at this website: www.med.nyu.edu/hjd/harkness.

> **Did you know**
> If you are tired, dehydrated or finding it difficult to concentrate, you are more likely to suffer an injury.

Dealing with injuries

It is possible that at some point a dancer might get injured in a dance session, and if this happens you need to know what to do. Obviously if you suspect there are any broken bones you need to consult the emergency services immediately, but if the injuries are limited to a sprain or strain then you should adopt the RICED procedure:

- **R**est – stop the activity.
- **I**ce – apply ice for 10 minutes at intervals for the first 24 hours to reduce pain and swelling. Ice should not be applied directly to the skin, but it can be crushed and wrapped in a wet towel, which can be held against the injury.
- **C**ompression – apply a moderately firm bandage over the affected area and all around it to help control swelling.
- **E**levation – raise the injury and keep it that way for 24 hours to improve the drainage of fluid and reduce the flow of blood to the area.
- **D**iagnosis – get a professional opinion if you are concerned about the injury.

> **Remember**
> A bag of peas or ice cubes covered with a damp cloth makes a good, inexpensive cold-pack.

> **Did you know**
> Good nutrition speeds recovery from injury.

3.4 Rehearsing safely – what should you wear?

Choosing what to wear for your dance class is really important. If you do not choose well it can adversely affect the way that you move and how you feel psychologically about your work.

> **Objectives**
>
> Explore what constitutes safe and appropriate clothing for rehearsal.
>
> Learn how to make informed choices about what you wear for a rehearsal.

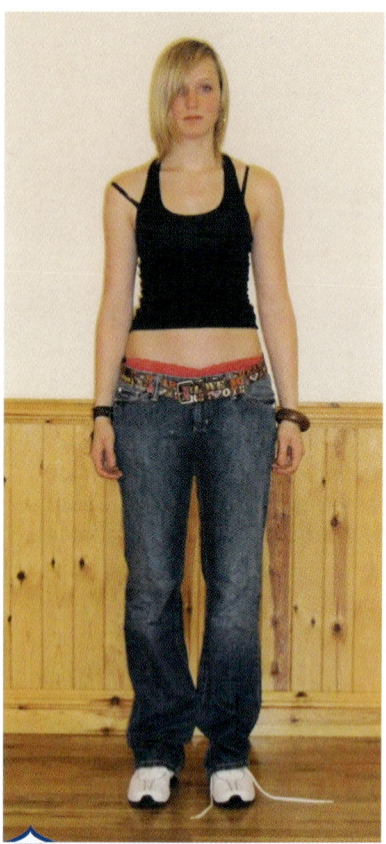

A Is this appropriate dress for a rehearsal?

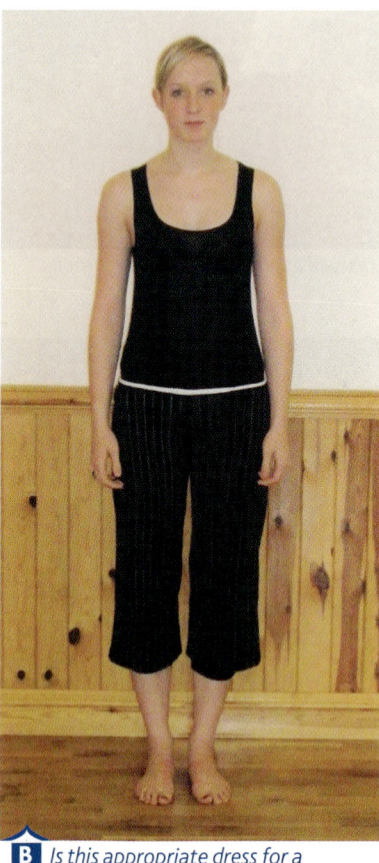

B Is this appropriate dress for a rehearsal?

Spot the difference

Look at the two images of the same dancer wearing different rehearsal clothes. Consider the differences between the images from both a health and safety and an aesthetic point of view.

With a partner, discuss the differences between the two images. You might like to think about the following points:

- When is it appropriate to wear clothing in layers?
- What advantages are there in using stretchy fabrics?
- What types of material would be suitable for dance clothing?
- Why do we need to make sure our dance-wear is clean?
- Why might we choose to wear loose but not baggy clothes?
- What are the advantages of dance-wear that gives good support and coverage to the body?

> **Key terms**
>
> **Aesthetic:** something we judge to be appealing and tasteful.
>
> **Risk assessment:** identification and assessment of potentially harmful factors.

Chapter 3 Safe dance practice

- Why do we need to make sure that trousers are not dragging on the floor?
- What factors influence our choice of appropriate footwear? Think about the suitability of bare feet, socks, trainers, ballet shoes, etc.
- Why is it considered dangerous to wear buckles, belts and jewellery in a dance class?
- What factors influence our choice of an appropriate hairstyle?

Activity

A **risk assessment** grid has been started for you below. See how many entries you can think of. Can you get 30?

C Risk assessment grid

	Item	Safe dance practice – yes or no?	Reason
1	Long trousers	No	The dancer may slip on the excess material and fall
2	Wide-leg trousers	No	The dancer might catch their foot in the excess material, causing them to trip
3	Top which covers the midriff	Yes	Keeps lower back warm and improves aesthetic appearance

AQA Examiner's tip

You will gain marks for being appropriately and safely dressed in both Unit 2 (Set dance) and Unit 3 (Performance in a duo/group dance).

Remember

What you wear to a dance class can affect your performance. You do not need to spend a fortune on designer clothes in order to look good, but it is worth giving some thought to what you wear so that you are able to work safely, comfortably and confidently.

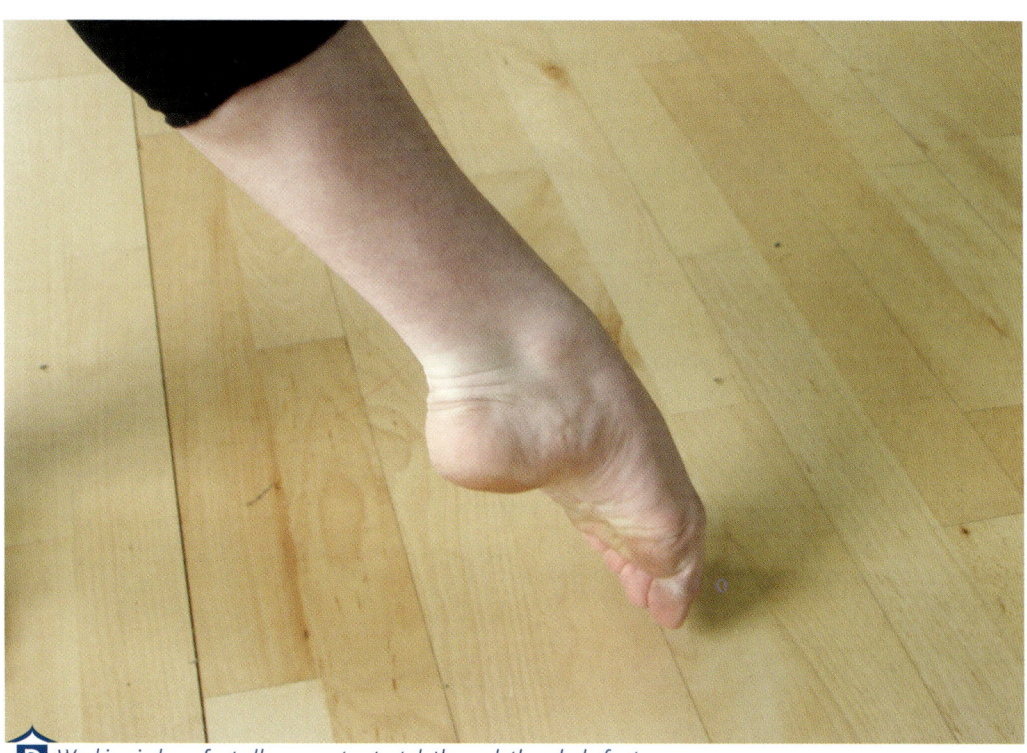

D Working in bare feet allows you to stretch through the whole foot to the ends of your toes

3.5 Rehearsing safely – what is in a space?

Safety first

Although often you cannot choose what space you rehearse in, it is really important to know what to look for to ensure that the space is safe to work in. Some of the things we need to consider are as follows:

- Is the studio big enough to accommodate the number of dancers rehearsing? They need to be able to work without bumping into the person next to them.
- Is the space high enough to accommodate lifts and jumps?
- Are there any obstructions in the room such as pillars? If so, have they been padded and marked in a bright colour as a safety precaution?
- Are there any other obstructions in the room that could be dangerous, such as chairs, other pieces of furniture or props? If so, can they be removed or put somewhere where they will not cause an obstruction?
- Is the floor surface appropriate? Is it splinter free, clean and smooth but not too slippery? Does it have some spring or bounce in it?
- Is the room temperature constant? The optimum safe temperature in a dance studio is 21°C. If the temperature falls below 18°C it is not safe to dance.
- Is there adequate ventilation in the room? There should be good draught-free circulation of fresh air, so an open window may not provide the best solution. What other solutions might there be?
- Is the studio well lit? Is the lighting even or are there dark spots?
- Are the mirrors made from safety glass and are the wall barres attached firmly to the wall?
- Are there any trailing wires, mats or other pieces of equipment that could cause a hazard to a dancer?

> **Objectives**
>
> Explore what constitutes a safe and appropriate space for rehearsal.
>
> Know how to decide if a particular studio is safe to rehearse in.

Activity

1. Look at Photo **A**, which shows a dance space. Obviously there are some things that you cannot tell from the image, such as the temperature of the room, but you can form some impression of its suitability as a dance space.
   a. How would you rate this as a suitable space for rehearsal?
   b. What things would you want to check out for yourself when you enter the space?
   c. Look on the internet for images of other dance rehearsal spaces and see how you rate those.

Chapter 3 Safe dance practice 31

A *Is this a suitable space for rehearsal?*

Activity

2 Using the list on the opposite page to guide you, carry out a risk assessment of one of the spaces that you rehearse in regularly. A simple format for a risk assessment grid is shown in Table **B**.

B *Sample risk assessment grid*

	Item	Description	Potential hazard	Action needed
1	Obstruction	Supporting pillars in the middle of the studio	Dancers could bump into them or fall against them and injure themselves	The pillars should be padded with a resilient material and marked in a bright colour
2	Temperature of room	17°C	Too cold. The dancers are more likely to pull muscles and serious injuries might occur	The space must be heated above 18°C before dance can take place

Remember

It is important that you are able to assess potential hazards in a space and that you take action to inform someone or deal with any problems yourself. If you cannot do this, you or someone else in the class may get injured.

Chapter summary

3

In this chapter you have learnt:

- ✔ what constitutes a good diet for a dancer
- ✔ the importance of keeping yourself hydrated
- ✔ what happens in a warm-up and cool-down and why we need to do these
- ✔ how to construct a good warm-up and cool-down
- ✔ how to perform dance safely
- ✔ how to deal with minor sprains and strains
- ✔ what to wear for dance
- ✔ what hazards to look for in a dance studio.

Revision quiz

1. What foodstuffs do dancers need to eat moderate quantities of?
2. What is lactic acid?
3. Why is it important for a dancer to sip water regularly?
4. Identify the three reasons why we need to warm up the body before exercise.
5. Why is a cool-down important?
6. What is a dynamic stretch?
7. What is another name for a jump?
8. Identify three things that you need to consider when carrying out movements that involve supporting and lifting a partner.
9. Why is it important to work slowly when you are planning new moves involving weight-sharing with a partner?
10. What does RICED mean?
11. If you do not have a cold-pack to put on a sprain, what can you use instead?
12. Name three things that you should avoid wearing in a dance class.
13. Identify three things you would look for when carrying out a risk assessment for a potential dance space.
14. What is the optimum safe temperature for a dance space?

A These dancers need to be very aware of safe practice in order to execute this move safely

4 The ingredients of dance

In this chapter you will learn about:

- actions, space, dynamics and relationships
- how to select and use actions, space, dynamics and relationships to increase movement vocabulary
- how to develop actions, space, dynamics and relationships for choreography.

Introduction

As you learn about creating, performing, analysing and directing dances, you will be introduced to some new vocabulary: words such as actions, space, dynamics and relationships. These are the ingredients of dance.

Why you need to understand the ingredients of dance

Understanding the ingredients of dance will help you to succeed in all areas of the course. As a dancer, you need to learn, understand and use technical and expressive skills to help improve your performances. As a choreographer, you need to develop an understanding of the words used to create and develop movement for dances. As a critic, you need to be able to describe and analyse movement, costumes, set designs, lighting and accompaniment and to interpret possible meanings of dances.

In this chapter you will learn how to choose actions, space, dynamics and relationships that are appropriate to the dance you are creating. You will have the chance to experiment by way of some practical activities and by observing and analysing some professional dance works.

A Students developing the ingredients of dance

4.1 Actions

What are actions?

Actions are **what** the body is doing. There are five main groups of actions: jump, turn, gesture, travel, and stillness or **balance**.

Jump

Jump describes the action of rising into the air using the muscles in the legs and feet. Jumps can be varied according to how you use your feet. For example, you can take off from two feet and land on two feet, or take off from one foot and land on the other foot. Think about other variations. You can change your body shape when you are in the air, for example by performing a star jump. You can also vary the height and length of the jump.

Turn

To turn means to move around an axis or to rotate.

Gesture

This is an action or movement that does not involve a transfer of weight from one body part to another. Nodding your head or waving your arms are examples of gestures.

Travel

Travelling means moving from one place to another. This action can be further divided into:

- stepping
- travelling on other parts of the body, for example sliding, crawling or cartwheeling.

Stillness or balance

Stillness is when the body is not moving; it is held in a still position. Stillness can be dynamic and last for a fraction of a second, or it can be a position that is held for much longer.

Diagram **B** is a mind map of some different types of actions. It is not a complete list and you could use the empty branches in the diagram to add other words that relate to actions. You will see that the different types of actions have been separated into three categories:

- stop and go
- body
- body percussion.

> **Objectives**
> Learn about different types of actions.
>
> Use actions appropriate to the theme of a dance.

> **Key terms**
> **Balance**: a steady or 'held' position.

A Stillness

Look at Diagram **B** carefully to make sure you understand the differences between each category of action. Aim to collect as many action words as you can throughout the course.

Basing actions on a dance theme

It is important to choose appropriate actions if you want your dance idea or theme to be effective. For example, if you are creating a dance based on the theme of 'trapped', you would probably choose a lot of gestures and stillness to help that dance idea come across. You would not look trapped if you were running and jumping all over the stage!

Activity

1. Study a short section of one of the professional works listed in the specification for AQA GCSE Dance.
   a. Write down all of the actions that you observe in your chosen section.
   b. Do you think the actions chosen by the choreographer help you to understand the theme of the dance? Give reasons for your answer.

AQA Examiner's tip

The use of stillness can have huge impact on a dance. In *Ghost Dances*, Christopher Bruce uses stillness brilliantly at the end of each section as a highlight and to show the audience that a life has been taken.

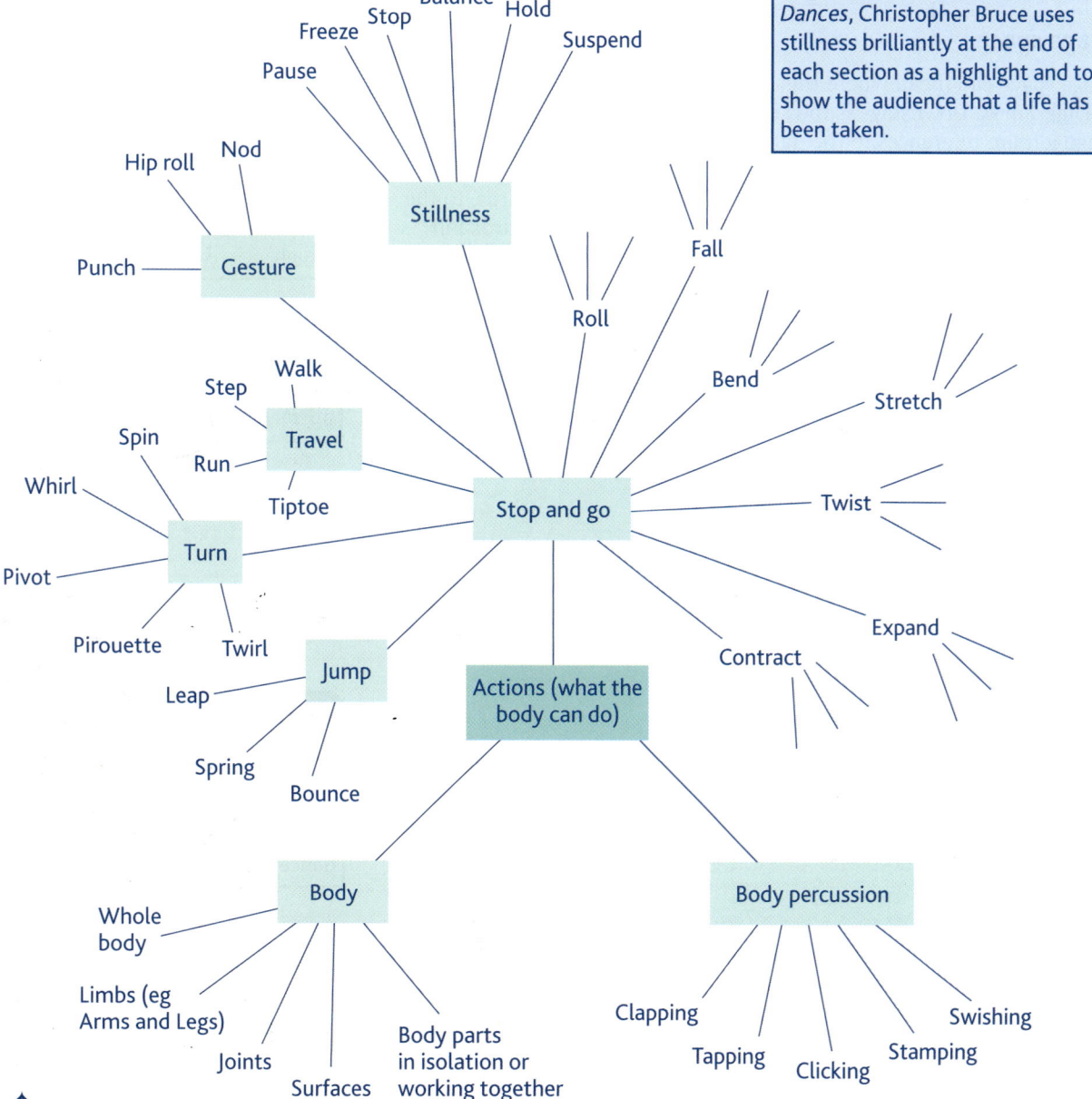

B Actions mind map

4.2 Space

What is space?

Space is **where** the body is moving. It can relate to:

- where a dancer is placed or where they move on a stage or in another performance space
- the direction in which the dancer is facing
- the pathways a dancer uses when travelling
- the **level** the dancer is on, for example on the floor or jumping
- the size and shape of a movement
- the size and patterns of group shapes.

Stage space

Stage space can mean where the dancer is placed on the stage. Look at Diagram **A**. Downstage is towards the audience and stage right and stage left are references to the dancer's right and left not that of the audience. Space also refers to the direction that a dancer is facing or moving in. The directions you can use are forwards, backwards, to the left, to the right, diagonally forwards right, diagonally forwards left, diagonally backwards right, diagonally backwards left, up and down.

> **Objectives**
> Understand different uses of space for dance.
>
> Learn how to use space when creating dances.

> **Key terms**
> **Level**: distance from the ground, for example low, medium or high.

> **Remember**
> Any area of the stage loses its power if it is overused.

A A stage plan with stage directions and indicating strong areas in the performance space

○ : Strong areas in order of power
---- : Powerful pathways

> **AQA Examiner's tip**
> Using space creatively, as with choosing actions, can help to make a dance idea very clear to an audience and it can give your dance visual impact.

Chapter 4 The ingredients of dance

Space mind map

- Pathways (on the floor; in the air)
  - Curved
  - Angular
  - Circular
  - Straight
- Proximity
  - Near
  - Far
- Levels
  - Low
  - Medium
  - High
- Personal
  - Around you/on the spot
- General
  - Around the room/performing space
- Size
  - Large
  - Small
- Body shape design
  - Asymmetrical
  - Symmetrical
  - Wide
  - Rounded
  - Narrow
  - Twisted
  - Angular
- Directions
  - Forwards
  - Backwards
  - Sideways
  - Diagonally
  - Up
  - Down

B Space mind map

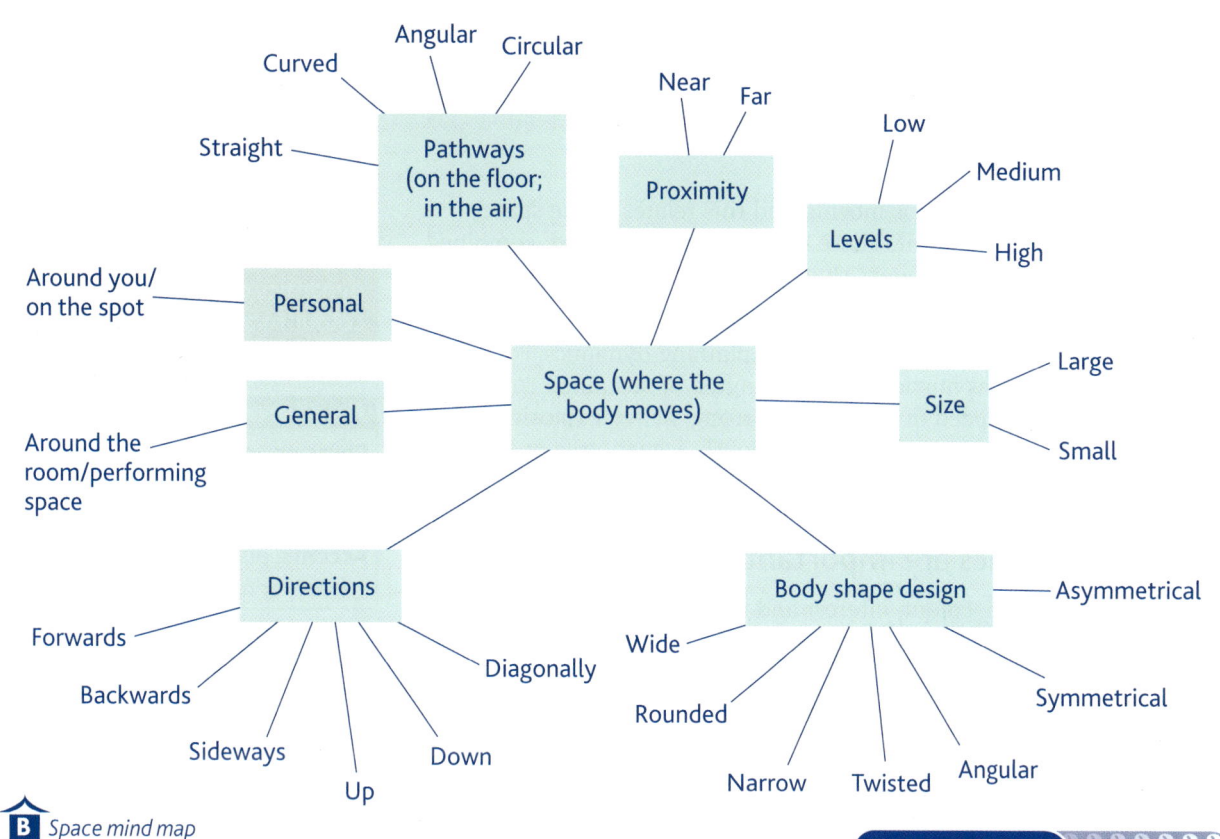

Activity

1 Work in groups of four. Take up the following starting position: three dancers are standing together in one area of the dance space with their backs turned to the fourth dancer, who is standing in a separate space.

- a Consider this spatial position as a starting point for a dance with the title 'Enemies'.
- b Choose three other spatial positions for the four dancers that would also suit this theme.
- c Choose actions that can take you from one position to the other.

Activity

2 Explore as many different travelling movements as you can, including rolling and crawling. For each type of travel, find a different pathway that is made in the performing space when travelling, for example a spiral, a diagonal line, a curve, a zigzag, a meandering pathway.

> **Did you know?**
> The terms 'upstage' and 'downstage' came about because a traditional stage sloped so that the audience had a better view. This meant that dancers literally had to move down the stage to be closer to the audience.

4.3 Dynamics

What are dynamics?

Dynamics are **how** the body is moving and this relates to the speed, energy and flow of movement. These elements can be varied, combined and contrasted to create different rhythms, **phrasing** and **accents** to movements.

Descriptive words tend to be used when explaining dynamics. For example, words such as hurried, speedy, languid or sustained could be used to describe the speed of movement. Strong, heavy, explosive or forceful could suggest the energy used. Smooth, jagged, free or bound could describe the flow of the movement.

Why dynamics are important in dance

Dynamics add texture, colour, interest and variety to a dance and can help to show the dance idea, the mood or the atmosphere of a dance more clearly. Dances that are slow and smooth throughout can become very boring to watch, while dances that are sharp, strong and fast throughout can confuse the audience. Another way to look at dynamics is in terms of fashion. If someone wears one colour from top to toe, the overall look can be a bit boring. If another person wears a pink and green spotted shirt with yellow and orange striped trousers and a red jacket, you would have to wear your sunglasses because it would be too much!

It is always a good idea to vary the dynamics in a dance work (and in fashion). You can see some examples of words describing dynamics in Diagram **A**, but feel free to add your own to the empty branches in the diagram as these are just examples and there are alternatives.

> **Objectives**
> Understand what dynamics are.
>
> Understand how different dynamics can add interest and colour to a dance.

> **Key terms**
> **Phrasing**: individual actions that are joined together make a phrase.
>
> **Accents**: placement of stress on beats or movements.

> **Activity**
>
> 1. Think how it would feel to do the following.
>   a. freefall
>   b. freeze and melt
>   c. fly high in the sky
>   d. walk on air
>   e. seize the moment
>   f. be overwhelmed with grief.

It takes practice to be able to show very clear dynamic contrasts.

> **Activity**
>
> 2. Choose a movement and perform it very quickly then slowly. Try to show a real dynamic contrast.

Chapter 4 The ingredients of dance

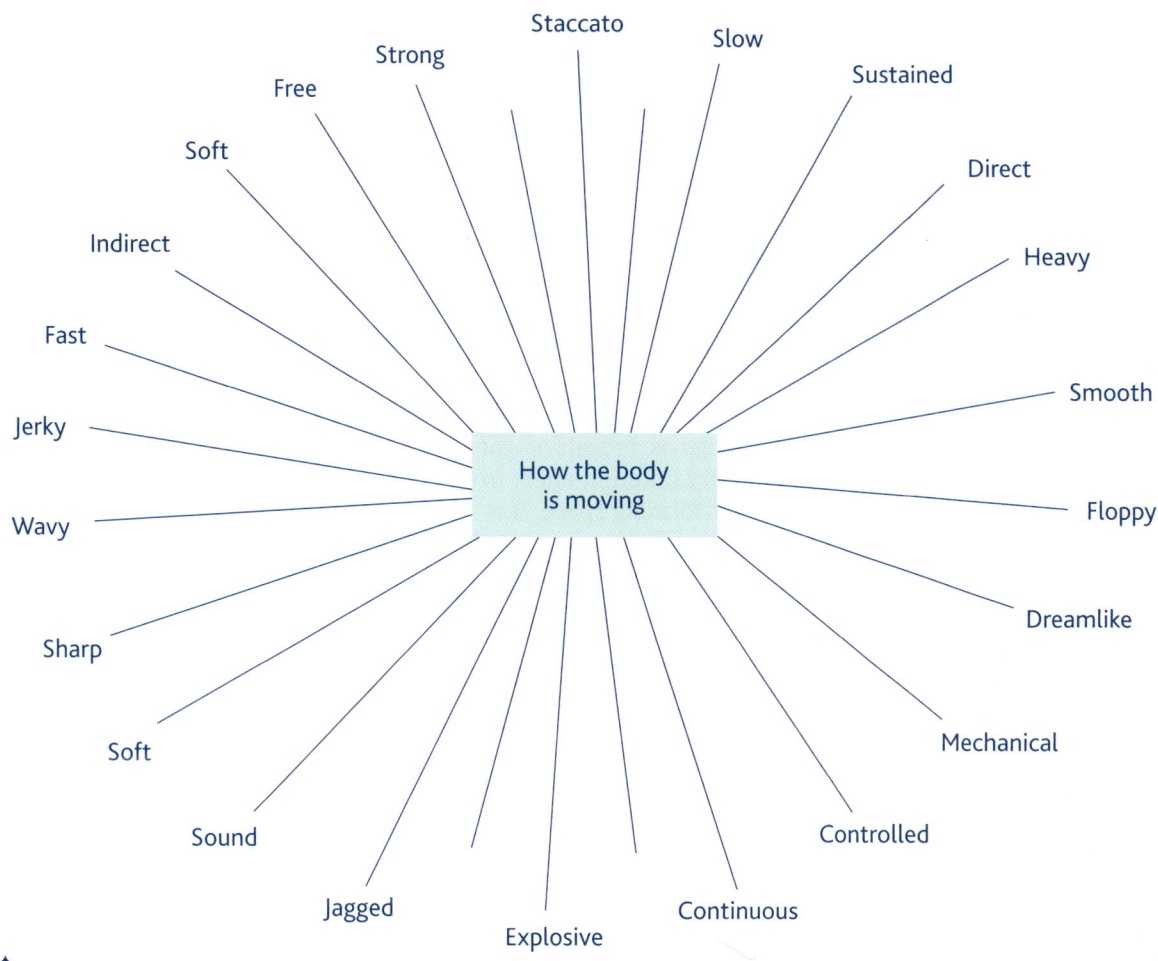

Dynamics mind map with central node "How the body is moving" branching to:
Staccato, Slow, Strong, Sustained, Free, Direct, Soft, Heavy, Indirect, Smooth, Fast, Floppy, Jerky, Dreamlike, Wavy, Mechanical, Sharp, Controlled, Soft, Continuous, Sound, Explosive, Jagged

A *Dynamics mind map*

Activities

3 Which dynamic qualities would be suitable for a dance based on machines?

4 Which dynamic qualities would be suitable for a dance based on the tango?

Hint

If you have mirrors in your dance classroom, use them to check if you can move using contrasting dynamics. Or ask a classmate or a teacher to observe you.

Activity

5 Think of a section of dance that you have created and/or performed in class time, perhaps for the set dance.
  a Dance the section.
  b Now describe the dynamics of each of the movements you have performed.
  c Perform the section again with different dynamics. Does it feel different? How? Discuss what differences you have found. Do the original dynamics of the section work better? Why do you think that is the case?

4.4 Relationships

What are relationships?

Relationships are about the way in which you dance with others. Varying the relationships throughout a dance adds visual interest and variety and can help to make a dance idea clear. For instance, dancing in unison can look powerful and communicate an idea of strength.

Types of dance relationships

Relationships can be developed in time and in space and through actions. Relationships in dance can also change as a result of using different numbers of dancers. A solo has a very different effect from having a group of dancers on the stage or performing space. If a prop is used in a piece of dance then a dancer could move towards or away from it, onto or off it, under or around it. This is also a type of relationship and you can see a good example of it in *Swansong* by Christopher Bruce, where a chair has many uses and is used by all of the dancers.

You will learn more about using dance relationships for choreography in Chapter 5, Creating dances. There are some simple examples of different dance relationships in Diagram **A**. Use the space provided to add other dance relationships.

Objectives

Understand dance relationships.

Learn how to use relationships effectively when creating dances.

Activity

1. Look at the photographs of duos and groups performing dances that appear throughout this book. Match the dance relationships you see to the terms in the mind map.

AQA Examiner's tip

It is important to be able to identify and understand actions, space, dynamics and relationships for your performance, choreography and written exams.

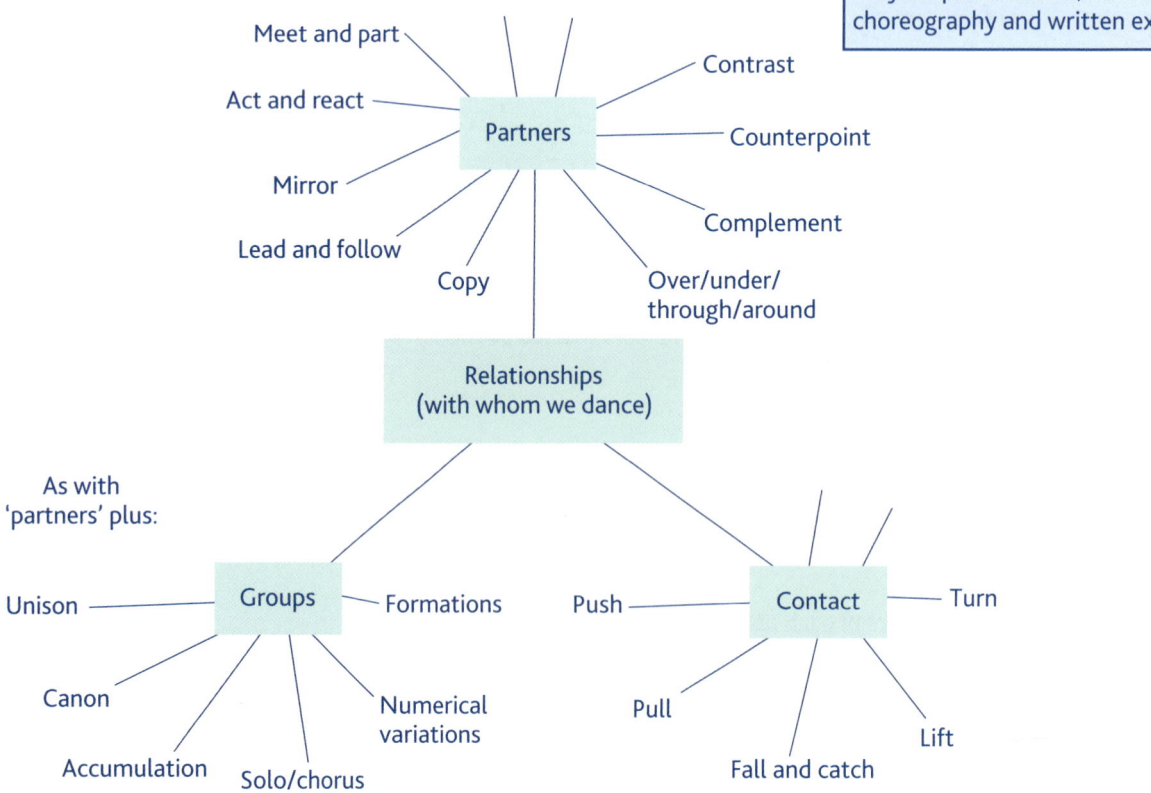

Relationships (with whom we dance)

- Partners
  - Meet and part
  - Act and react
  - Mirror
  - Lead and follow
  - Copy
  - Over/under/through/around
  - Complement
  - Counterpoint
  - Contrast
- Groups (As with 'partners' plus:)
  - Unison
  - Canon
  - Accumulation
  - Solo/chorus
  - Numerical variations
  - Formations
- Contact
  - Push
  - Pull
  - Fall and catch
  - Lift
  - Turn

A Relationships mind map

Chapter 4 The ingredients of dance 41

Activity

2 Look at the actions of the men's opening duet of *Overdrive* by Richard Alston (Chapter 1).
  a Choose six actions from the section and add them together to make a short phrase.
  b Rehearse it in unison.
  c Now apply other relationships that you have learned.
  d Does the addition of other relationships add interest to the phrase?

B *Dancers showing complementary relationships in* Rosas Danst Rosas

Extension activity

Learn the opening phrase of section 1 of *Overdrive*, being as accurate with the actions, dynamics, space and relationships as you can. If you watch/listen to the studio demonstration of section 1, Alston describes the dance as being fast and driven but laid back. This makes you think about using all four 'ingredients' of dance: actions, space, dynamics and relationships.

We have explored the idea of actions, space, dynamics and relationships being the ingredients of dance, so try the next activity to create a dance from a 'recipe'.

Activities

3 Create a sequence based on the idea of a sizzling stir-fry. Explore the following actions: slice, chop, stir, pour, sprinkle, drop and slide.

4 In groups of 3–5, experiment with other actions that you could use when making a stir-fry.

5 Select the actions that work best and put them in the order that you would prepare a stir-fry.

6 Add suitable dynamics.

7 Decide how you will use space.

8 Think about using a variety of group relationships.

C *Dancers showing contact in* Perfect

Remember

The maximum number of dancers in your performance and choreography is five.

Chapter summary

4

In this chapter you have learnt:
In this chapter you have been introduced to the basic principles of dance vocabulary that include actions, space, dynamics and relationships. Remember that actions mean **what** the body is doing, space means **where** the body is moving, dynamics means **how** the body is moving (quality), and relationships means **with whom** you are moving.

■ Check your understanding
It is important to know and understand the differences between actions, space, dynamics and relationships and to be able to describe and analyse them in your own performance and choreography dances as well as in professional dance works. Try the activity below to check your understanding.

Activity

1 You will need a blank sheet of A4 paper, a pen or pencil, a video or DVD of one of the professional works you are studying.
  a Divide your sheet of paper into four and label the quarters Actions, Space, Dynamics and Relationships.
  b Watch a section of one of the professional works that you will be studying for your GCSE Dance course.
  c As you watch your chosen section, record your observations in the appropriate boxes.
  d Check with your teacher or another student to see if you answered correctly.

You may have to watch the dance work several times before you attempt this task because analysing movement is not easy.

Now that you understand what actions, space, dynamics and relationships are, apply your knowledge to the following practical task.

Extension activity

You are the choreographer of a dance called 'No Way Out'.

1 Create a short phrase using appropriate actions, space, dynamics and relationships.

2 Tell your dancers the reasons for your choices.

3 Did your actions, space, dynamics and relationships choices suit the theme of the dance? Give reasons for your answer.

kerboodle!

5 Creating dances

43

In this chapter you will learn about:

- the process of creating dances (choreography)
- exploring and communicating ideas in dance
- creating, selecting and organising dance material
- shaping and structuring dances.

Key terms

Aural setting: audible accompaniment to the dance such as music, words, song, soundscape, etc.

AQA Examiner's tip

The choreography for a solo or group carries the most marks of all the assessed tasks (25 per cent) so you will need plenty of practice and time in order to be a really successful choreographer.

Getting creative

The importance of choreography

Whether you are creating your own work, performing dances created by others or looking at professional works, you need to have a good knowledge and understanding of the process of choreography.

This chapter focuses on the choreographic tools that you need, including:

- where to get ideas and starting points (stimuli) for a dance
- working with a stimulus
- choosing and using accompaniment (**aural setting**)
- selecting and developing movements
- choreographing dance for more than one dancer
- organising dance material
- shaping and structuring dances.

What makes a good choreography?

Your final choreography for a solo or group provides you with an opportunity to say what you want in the way that you want it through the powerful medium of movement. Look at the description of a very good choreography from the AQA GCSE Dance specification and think about what you will need to do to achieve success:

'The candidate shows an inspired and original response to the stimulus or starting point. The selection of action, dynamic, spatial and where appropriate, relationships content, is original, well-realised and varied, adding significance and interest to the dance idea and enhancing artistic intent. The overall structure is highly appropriate and very effective in giving unity to the piece. The candidate makes highly effective use of a range of choreographic devices and principles and the choice of aural setting is highly appropriate and insightful. The mood and meaning of the dance is communicated in a highly sensitive manner.'

Starter activity

Look at the description of a very good choreography taken from the AQA GCSE Dance specification. Highlight any words whose meaning you do not understand. Find out what they mean by talking to your teacher and friends, and by looking through the rest of this chapter.

5.1 Choosing a stimulus

What is a stimulus?

A stimulus is something that inspires you to create dances. It provides a starting point for you to explore movement ideas. All artists respond to the world around them, whether they use movement, sound, images or words. Some artists have very important and serious messages to communicate, while others just enjoy playing with material and the ideas they generate. You can stick very closely to the stimulus or starting point, using it to guide and shape the material, or your dance might develop in a different direction once the stimulus has done its job of getting you started.

Why are stimuli important?

It is important that you experience lots of different stimuli – it will help you to develop your creative and problem-solving skills and originality. Using different stimuli will help you to find new ways of moving and it will also help you to appreciate the dances you watch. For your final choreography you will be awarded marks for your 'creative and imaginative response to the selected stimulus/starting point' (AQA GCSE Dance specification).

Different types of stimuli

Stimuli can be grouped in ways that link to the senses: visual (sight), auditory (sound), kinaesthetic (feeling), tactile (touch) and ideational (the brain). Look in the fact file (see Chapter 9, Professional works fact file, on page 116) for the different stimuli or starting points used for each dance featured. What type of stimulus is each?

For your assessed choreography you have the following list of stimuli to choose from.

Words, a poem or a piece of text

This could be instructions, plays, recipes, newspaper reports, speeches, random words or phrases, stories, etc.

Think about the meaning, story line, **character**, rhythm, sound, phrasing, etc.

Martin Luther King's famous speech was the stimulus for *Longevity*, choreographed by Gary Lambert for the Phoenix Dance Company. The choreographer interpreted images and phrases from the speech, the rhythm and phrasing of words and the emotional content in this moving duo.

A photograph or a piece of 2D or 3D art

This could be drawings, paintings, sculptures, collages, cartoons, prints, photos, etc.

Think about people, places, objects, associations, line, shape, form, colour, texture, pattern, **abstract**, representational, etc.

In *Tag* by Jonzi D, the dancers represent the abstract shapes and lines of graffiti.

Objectives

Learn about the different types of stimuli and what to look for.

Learn what inspires professional choreographers.

Key terms

Character: a role or part expressed by a dancer.

Abstract: actions or features that denote the quality or essence of the original.

AQA Examiner's tip

Rather than use a 'big' theme such as 'water', focus on a more specific idea such as a 'river journey'.

Remember

Look for a stimulus (and what really interests you) in other subjects you are studying – poems in English, paintings in Art and Design, physical features in Geography, characters and events in History.

A How might the shapes and patterns in this painting by Joan Miró stimulate dance ideas?

A prop

For example a suitcase, umbrella, overcoat, hat, broom, piece of rope, scarf, piece of Lycra or a sheet.

Think about the texture, shape, size, movement, meaning, mood, character, sound.

Gene Kelly uses an umbrella as a prop in a fantastic variety of ways in his famous *Singin' in the Rain* solo.

A feature of the natural world

For example a landscape, seascape, rainforest, weather, earthquake, volcano, earth, air, fire or water.

Think about the shape, form, movement, pattern, journeys, effects on living things.

Siobhan Davies's *Wyoming* was inspired by the American landscape, sky and climate.

A piece of music composed before 1970

For example instrumental, sung, classical, pop, solo, orchestral or quartet.

Think about the style, time, place, culture, form/ structure, tempo, mood, melody, meaning, pattern, rhythm, lyrics.

B *Gene Kelly provided the choreography for* Singin' in the Rain

Front Line by Henri Oguike was inspired by Shostakovitch's *String Quartet No. 9*. Oguike used the dynamics, rhythm and mood of the music as well as the musical manuscript to create dance material.

An everyday activity; a topical or historical event

This could be people at work, rest or play; places where people gather; routines and rituals; news items; dramas and conflicts; events that changed the world, and so forth.

Think about human behaviour, movement patterns, groupings, formations, interaction, mood.

An example is the way in which Matthew Bourne choreographs waving and saluting gestures in the first act of *Swan Lake*.

Activities

1. In pairs, write down the instructions for tying a shoelace (for example, pull apart, cross over, loop round, etc.). Use the key words in the same order to create a duo.

2. Listen carefully to a rock 'n' roll song such as *Blue Suede Shoes* by Carl Perkins. Use the structure, style, mood and lyrics to plan a class dance.

Hint

Keep a dance ideas scrapbook. Collect pictures, news items and scraps of information that grab your interest.

AQA Examiner's tip

One dance idea can use different types of stimulus. For a dance based on clouds, your stimuli could include shape and movement from observations (natural); photos or films of different types and formations (visual) and Rupert Brooke's poem *Clouds* (auditory).

links

Refer to Chapter 9, Professional works fact file (pages 116–125).

5.2 How to use a stimulus

■ Progressing your idea for a dance

So, you have an idea for your dance, what next? If you were going to bake a cake, you would probably consult a recipe and this would tell you what ingredients to collect before you start. Consider this as the stage where you are creating a recipe for your dance. You need to decide what ingredients to use long before you go into the studio so that you have a collection of things that work together. These should provide the ideas so that you can experiment with different movements to create a bank of material you can develop and refine.

Imagine you have decided to do a dance about an everyday activity and you have chosen to interpret the boiling of a kettle. The dance is going to be about cold water being poured into the kettle, which is then heated up to boiling point, and gradually cools when the kettle is switched off.

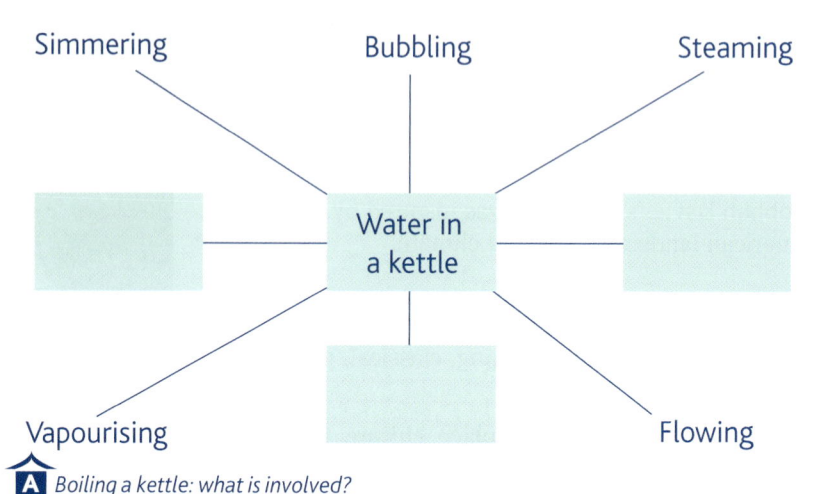

Objectives
Plan your dance before you start working on the movement material.

Spider diagram – Water in a kettle: Simmering, Bubbling, Steaming, Vapourising, Flowing (with blank spaces for additional words)

A Boiling a kettle: what is involved?

Activity

Diagram **A** is a spider diagram of words associated with the theme of boiling a kettle. Can you think of other words to include? Add them to the spider diagram in the spaces provided and draw in more branches if necessary.

Make a spider diagram of words associated with your theme. These words will help you with ideas for the dynamics and the action content of your dance later on.

Key terms
Climax: the most important or significant moment of the dance, which usually happens near the end.

■ Planning your dance

Diagram **B** is an example of a dance planner. You can copy the layout shown or come up with your own format. The great thing about dance planners is that you can work on planning your dance in your bedroom or in a classroom. Then, when you get to do some practical work in the studio, you will be able to make the best use of your time because you have already thought about the plan. By the time you have completed your own dance planner you should have a good idea how to start creating your dance. Think about the structure for your dance too; this is often suggested by the subject matter.

Getting started on your dance is the hardest part, but doing some forward planning will help you to avoid a situation where you get into the studio and then end up standing there hoping desperately for inspiration. The reality is that inspiration will probably not come – so get planning beforehand.

Hint
Try to think of a good title for your dance. It should be punchy and give a quick insight into what the dance is about. For example, your kettle dance could be called 'Boiling point'. This could be referenced in the **climax** of the dance. In this example, the climax of the dance would be when boiling point is reached.

Chapter 5 Creating dances 47

The dance idea

What kind of movements/motifs/phrases/ will the dance contain?

Structure of the dance

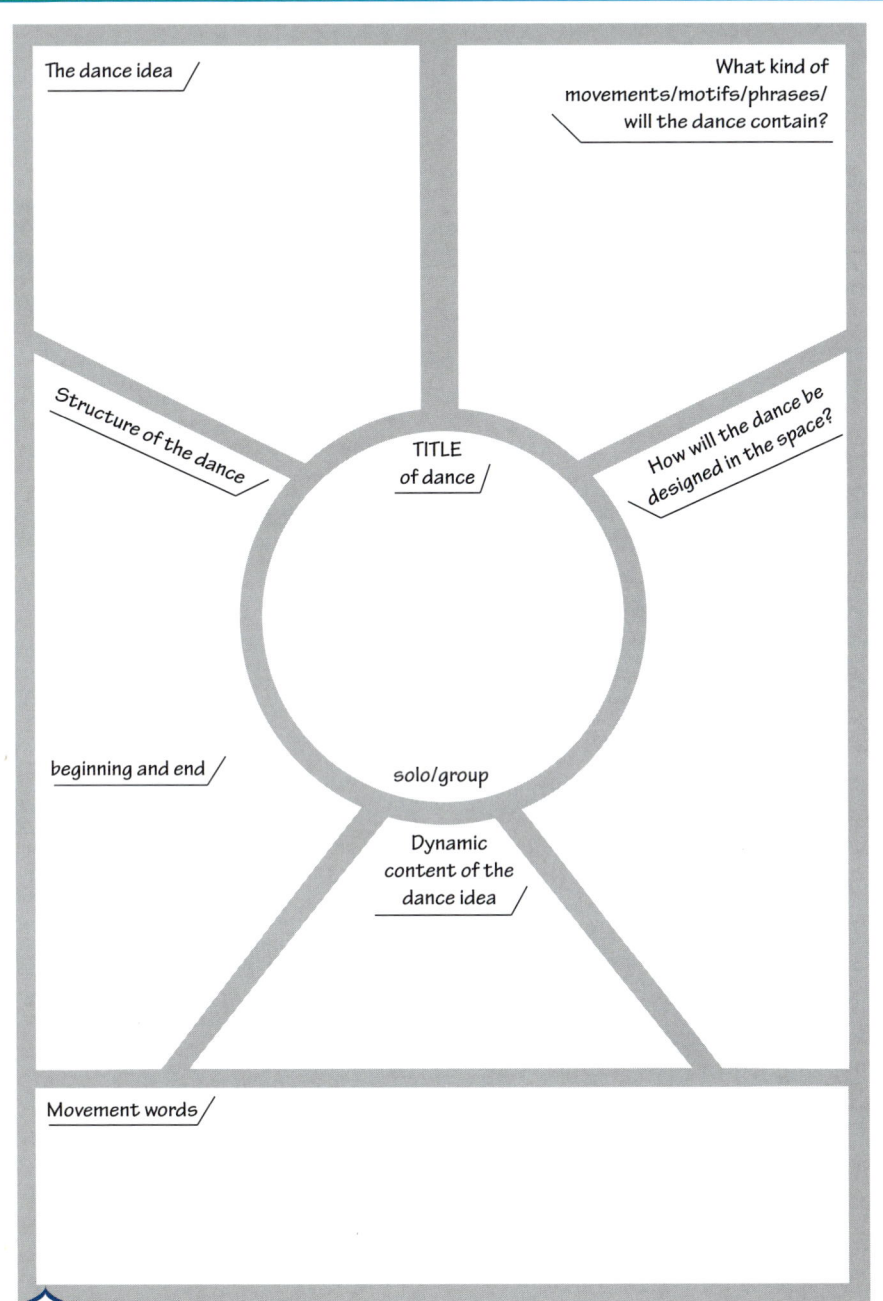

TITLE of dance

How will the dance be designed in the space?

beginning and end

solo/group

Dynamic content of the dance idea

Movement words

B An example of a dance planner

Activity

2 Use the dance planner and the painting in Photo **C** by Kandinsky to create a choreographic plan. You will need to decide if your ideas best lend themselves to a solo or group dance.

AQA Examiner's tip

Do not worry about what music you are going to use. It is often better to work the idea first and then find the music later. That way your idea, rather than the music, will drive your choreography.

C On White II, Kandinsky, 1923

5.3 Motif and development

What is a motif?

A motif is a movement or **phrase** of movements that embodies the style and content of a dance. It can be manipulated and developed in many different ways. A motif generally consists of actions and has a dynamic quality and spatial design. It can be as simple as a spiral – performed as a turn with arm gestures, then as a travelling pathway and finally as a group shape.

Why are motifs important?

Motifs are essential ingredients that can be repeated, varied and developed to help structure and organise a dance. A two- to three-minute dance will contain a number of motifs (try to create at least three in your dance). Motifs are also helpful to the audience because they clearly communicate the style and meaning of the dance and help the audience to process what they see. Motifs are used in art and music too. In Miró's painting on page 44, repeated and developed motifs include eyes, stars, spirals and discs.

Once you have a good grasp of motifs you are well on your way to being a good choreographer. You will be assessed on how effectively you develop and link motifs in your solo **composition** and on how successfully you select and structure material to communicate your idea in your main choreography.

> **Objectives**
> Recognise motifs.
> Know how to create and develop motifs.

> **Key terms**
> **Phrase**: a sequence of linked movements.
> **Composition**: a dance.

Recognising motifs

The central solo for *Bird Song* has a key motif that is repeated and developed. It consists of the torso arching and the arms lifting above the head as if the lungs are expanding. In this motif, movement and sound (the call of the Pied Butcher bird) become one. Think of one of the set dances that you have learned (or look at the DVD) and identify key movements and phrases that are repeated and developed.

In *Ghost Dances*, the following motifs in section two (Huajra) are repeated and developed later in section six (Sicuriadas):

- plié in parallel with arms reaching forward
- walks with heels leading and clear changes of direction
- dancers travelling in a line
- dynamic jumps in which the arms circle
- small triplet steps.

How to develop a motif (group)

You can develop motifs in a group in exactly the same way as for a solo, but you have more opportunities to vary the body, actions, dynamics and space between dancers. You can also develop the relationships in time and space and the use of number (see Diagram **A**).

Chapter 5 Creating dances

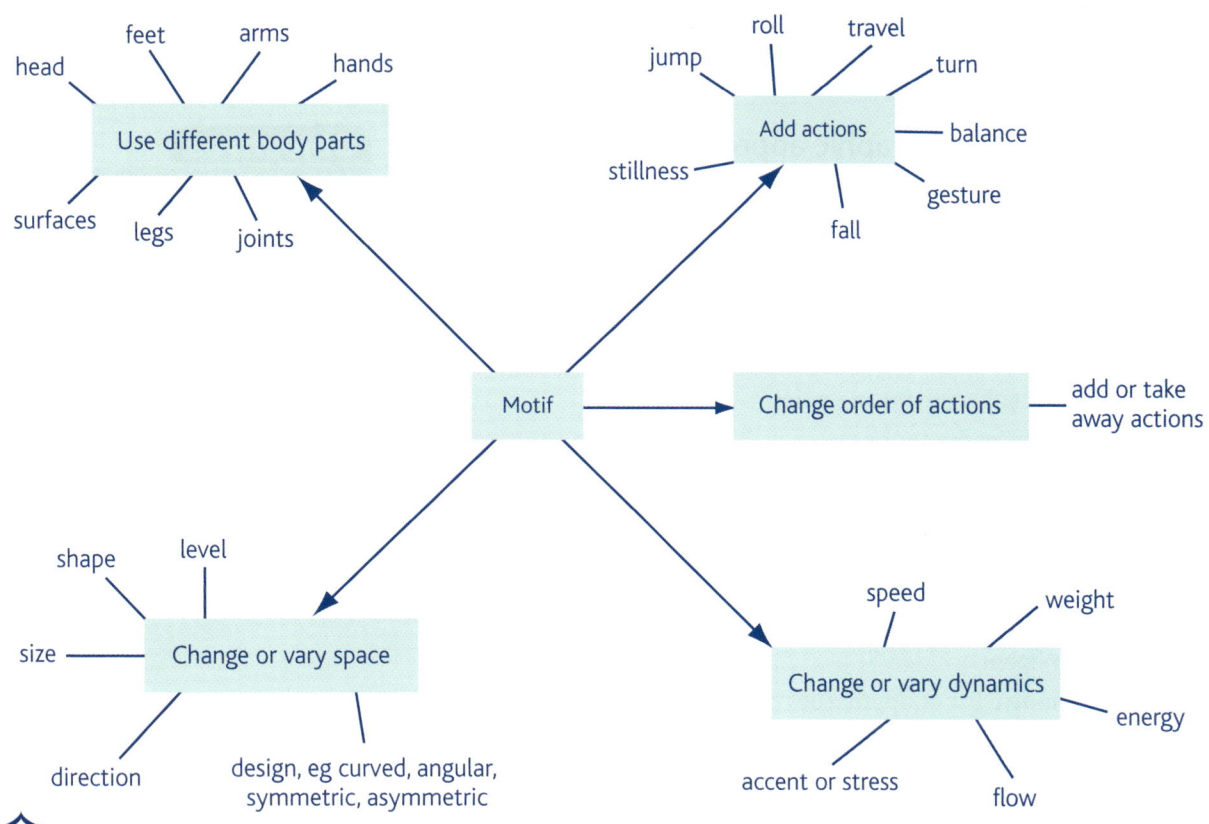

Motif development diagram

Use different body parts: head, feet, arms, hands, joints, legs, surfaces

Add actions: jump, roll, travel, turn, balance, gesture, fall, stillness

Change order of actions: add or take away actions

Change or vary space: shape, level, size, direction, design, eg curved, angular, symmetric, asymmetric

Change or vary dynamics: speed, weight, energy, flow, accent or stress

A Ways in which a motif can be developed

Activity

1 Select three letters (your 'tag' or initials) and draw them in the air with one hand. Use as much space as you can. Make sure you have clear action, dynamic and spatial content.
  a Draw the tag with three different body parts – the dynamic and spatial aspects might have to change to accommodate this.
  b Take an action away and add some more actions, for example jump, travel, roll, fall.
  c Vary the use of space, for example change level, direction, size.
  d Vary the dynamics, for example change the speed, weight, energy, flow.

Having carried out this activity, you will have created an initial motif (stage 2) and developed it in three different ways (stages 3–5). Or you will have created an initial motif (stage 2) and developed it in a complex way (using aspects of stages 3–5).

Activity

2 Using your 'tag' motifs, create a trio in which:
  a you all perform the same motif(s) as each other
  b you all perform your own motifs at the same time
  c one dancer performs their signature motif whilst the others perform a developed version of the same motif.

5.4 Choosing a choreographic approach

What is a choreographic approach?

A choreographic approach comprises two aspects:

- The creation of the dance material.
- The organisation of the dance material.

How you approach your choreography depends on several factors including:

- The type of stimulus or starting point.
- The theme, subject matter or message that you want to communicate.
- The way in which you create material with your dancers.
- The type of movement you use.
- The outcome you want to achieve – how you want the audience to feel.
- How the choreography relates to other aspects of production, such as accompaniment.

There is no definitive list of approaches to choreography, but we will look more closely at three in particular.

Contact improvisation

This is a way of making dance that usually involves two people exploring different ways of taking each other's weight. In this way you can develop a dance vocabulary and explore the physical relationship through actions such as push, pull, lean, lift, catch and throw. The resulting effect is weighty and relaxed as well as energetic and dynamic and it is often emotionally powerful. **Contact improvisation** challenges the traditional roles played by men and women in partner dances and often embraces other forms of movement such as martial arts. Works by Siobhan Davies and Motionhouse provide good examples of this approach.

Chance

This approach works well when movement itself is a starting point for a dance. It might include a random selection of movements and aspects of time and space, which will result in **chance** relationships between dancers. It requires good problem-solving skills in order to avoid total chaos. A true chance dance will mean that it is different every time, so it is best avoided for your final choreography. However, it is an approach that can be used to start the choreographic process. Numbers, dice, playing cards, flash cards and so on could be used to decide on the actions, the order and the directions dancers take. Chance is an approach associated with the American choreographer Merce Cunningham, who in turn has influenced Siobhan Davies and Richard Alston.

Collage

This is a way of organising the material and piecing together the dance ideas that you have created. It could include a number of choreographic

> **Objectives**
> Learn about the different approaches that you can take to make and organise dance material.

> **Key terms**
> **Contact improvisation**: work is created through weight-taking, etc.
> **Chance**: a method of choreography in which dance material is determined or manipulated using a random method, for example by throwing dice.
> **Literal**: actions or features that closely represent the subject, theme or idea.
> **Symbolic**: actions or features that suggest or convey an idea, theme or feeling, for example the thumbs up gesture.

techniques and approaches. There is no story line as such and the central theme is the unifying factor. A collage approach to the idea/theme of 'Time' could include: movements that suggest parts of a clock; contrasts in speed; and everyday actions used by people in a hurry. To some extent *Perfect* by Kevin Finnan and Motionhouse represents a collage approach.

What type of movement should you use?

It is important to consider the type of movements that best communicate your idea/theme. These could be **literal**, **symbolic** or abstract. The example given above for 'Time' uses all three. A different example can be seen in Table **A**.

A *Communicating the theme of journeys*

Literal (or representational)	Symbolic	Abstract
Passing through the ticket barrier	Following pathways	Two dancers pull, push, lift and manipulate each other across the space
Travelling on the escalator	Creating obstacles for each other to get over/under/around	
Waiting for a train		
Pushing to get on		
Holding on to the handrail		

What outcome do you want to achieve?

Think about how you want the audience to feel when they watch your choreography. Do you want them to laugh, cry, feel calm, be excited, entertained, intrigued or thoughtful? Consider the kind of dance that will achieve the outcome(s) you want.

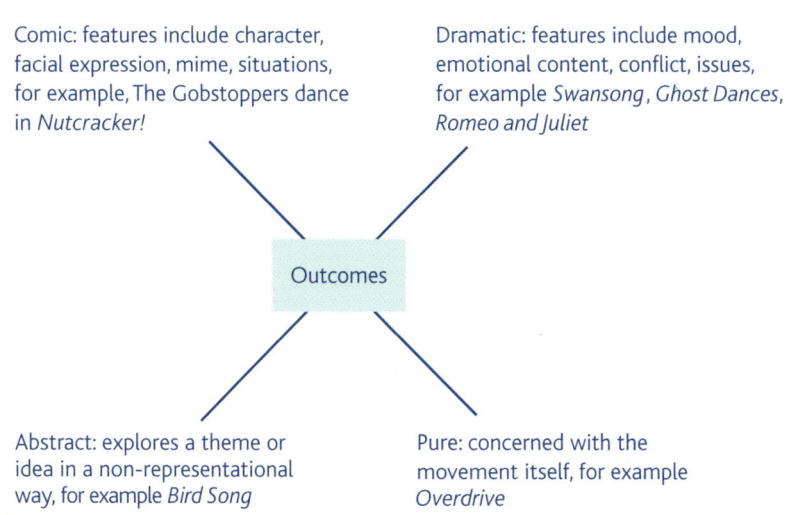

Activity

1. Look at the different ways in which choreographers such as Matthew Bourne, David Bintley and Frederick Ashton explore the theme of animals in dance.
   a. Research an animal that interests you (features, movements, behaviour, environment, etc.).
   b. Create a short literal study.
   c. Develop it to make it abstract.
   d. Which is most effective? Why?

links
Refer to Chapter 2 on distinctive choreographic styles.

AQA Examiner's tip
Always have the audience in mind when you choreograph a dance. This will help you be clear about what and how you communicate.

Comic: features include character, facial expression, mime, situations, for example, The Gobstoppers dance in *Nutcracker!*

Dramatic: features include mood, emotional content, conflict, issues, for example *Swansong*, *Ghost Dances*, *Romeo and Juliet*

Outcomes

Abstract: explores a theme or idea in a non-representational way, for example *Bird Song*

Pure: concerned with the movement itself, for example *Overdrive*

B *Possible outcomes for dance*

5.5 Choreographic devices

Choreographic devices are chosen by a choreographer to give dances depth of interest. You should explore a range of these devices when you create your solo composition and final choreography. Below are some examples of choreographic devices that you can try with the material you create.

Repetition

Repetition is a very simple choreographic device where you repeat all or part of one or more motifs that you have created. It helps you to reinforce ideas and it assists the audience in remembering certain movements. Be careful not to use this device too much as it can make a dance predictable and boring to watch.

Contrast

Contrast is where you add something completely different to the motifs or material you have created so far. For example, if your dance consists of slow, smooth movements on the spot, you could add a sharp, fast, travelling section to create a contrast in both the dynamic quality and the use of space.

Transitions

Transitions are the links between movements, phrases and sections of a piece of choreography. These are important as they should feel like they are part of the overall dance and not 'add-ons'. In *Rosas Danst Rosas* by Anne Teresa De Keersmaeker, the dancers link each section of the dance by moving from one space to another. As they do this they repeat the sharp turning motif they have used earlier so the transition from one section to the other feels natural, as if we have seen it before.

Highlights

Highlights are important moments (there can be more than one) in choreography where you are drawing the audience's attention to specific movements, held positions or even phrases within the choreography. These are usually the moments that the audience will remember most clearly after watching the choreography, so usually a choreographer would use highlights to make the starting point/ stimulus as clear as possible. To create a highlight in a dance you could, for example, build the dynamics and then pause. This is used very effectively in *Ghost Dances* by Christopher Bruce where the music and the movement build up towards the end of each section as the ghosts appear. The ghosts then lift the dancers as the music stops suddenly. This shows the audience that death has taken place – the message of the dance.

> **Objectives**
>
> Learn about different types of choreographic devices.
>
> Understand how choreographic devices help to structure choreography.

> **Key terms**
>
> **Repetition**: performing the same action or phrase again.
>
> **Transitions**: links between dance phrases or sections.
>
> **Highlights**: moments in the dance which draw attention to or emphasise something important.

Beginning and end

It is important to grab the audience's attention by choreographing an interesting and catchy beginning and end to your choreography. Think very carefully about how you want to begin and end your dance. Consider the starting and finishing positions, where the dancers are placed in the space, and entrances and exits. Do you want to build your dance idea up slowly? If so then you might want to extend the beginning of your choreography so that the audience can be drawn in to it gradually. Try the activity here to aid your understanding of this.

Activity

1. Imagine that you are choreographing a dance called 'Preparing for battle'.
   a. How long do you think the beginning of the dance would be?
   b. Would the ending of your dance be longer or shorter than the beginning?
   c. Create a short group dance and experiment with a long beginning/short ending and a short beginning/long ending. Which do you think is the most effective? Give reasons to support your point of view.

Climax

The climax is the high point of the dance, so you should choreograph your dance to lead to this moment. It could include an element of surprise for the audience. Siobhan Davies uses climax in an interesting way in *Bird Song*. The central solo is the starting point/stimulus for the work and was the first section to be choreographed, although it is in the middle of the dance. To build towards the climax, the sound score of *Bird Song* gradually becomes quieter in the sections leading to this solo, so the audience becomes aware that something important is about to happen.

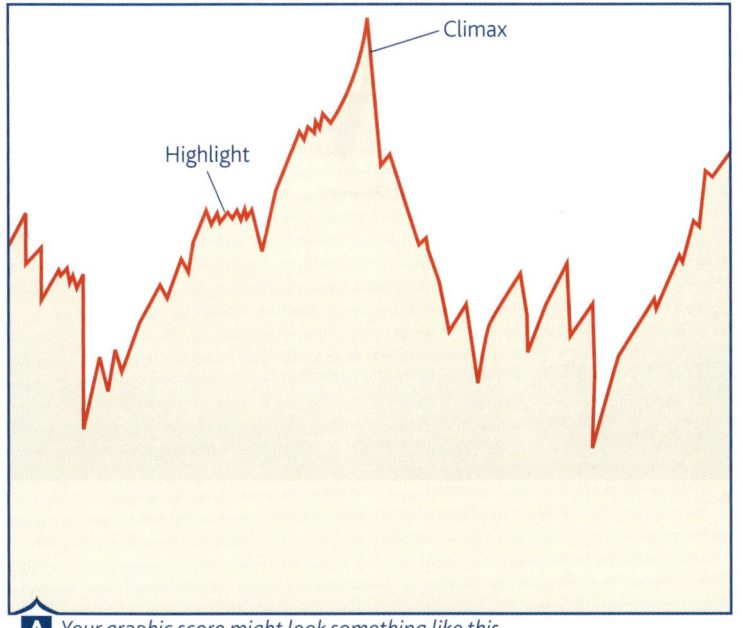

AQA Examiner's tip

As the ending of your dance is important, give it some thought rather than just letting it come to an abrupt stop. Don't leave the ending until the end.

Activity

2. Think of a short dance that you know well and create a graphic score (or 'temperature chart') to show the overall shape, highlights and climax. (See Diagram **A**.)

Remember

The end of a dance is probably the most important part, so have a very clear idea of the last image you want to leave the audience with. Avoid using the centre of the stage or lying down on the floor – they are far too obvious.

links

See motif and development on pages 48–49.

A *Your graphic score might look something like this*

5.6 Dance relationships

What are dance relationships?

You can make choices about relationships (that is, the connections and associations between a number of dancers) when you organise a group of dancers in time and space. Varying the relationships throughout a dance adds interest and variety, and can help make a dance idea or the meaning clearer. For instance, using unison can show an idea of power and strength. The ballroom scene in *Romeo and Juliet*, where the dancers perform a stately partner dance in unison, is a good example of this. Below are some examples of dance relationships.

> **Objectives**
>
> Learn about different dance relationships.
>
> Understand how to use dance relationships effectively in choreography.

Unison

This is where all dancers in the group perform the same movement at the same time, as you can see in Photo **A** of *Rosas Danst Rosas*. There are other types of unison where the dancers may not perform exactly the same actions, but the timing is the same. Overuse of unison weakens a dance, but it can be used very effectively to create a highlight or climax.

A *An example of unison, performed in* Rosas Danst Rosas

Activity

1 Look at the opening duet of *Overdrive* by Richard Alston.
  a Choose six actions from the section and add them together to make a short phrase.
  b Try to match the dynamics of Section 1 in *Overdrive*.
  c Rehearse side-by-side and in unison.
  d What do dancers have to focus on in order to achieve unison?

Canon

Canon is where one or more dancers move after each other. Simple canon is where a dancer dances an entire motif which is then followed by another dancer and so on. This can be made to look more effective by having the dancers overlap rather than wait until one dancer completes a motif before the next dancer begins. Dancers can perform the motif at the same time, but start at different points within the motif. You can see this in the final section of *Front Line* by Henri Oguike, where the dancers are all repeating the section where they slap their feet and gradually raise their arms above their heads. They are all dancing the same phrase but start dancing it at different moments in the motif.

Mirror image

This is similar to unison, but in this case one or more dancers use the other side of the body or travel in the opposite direction to create a mirror-type effect. This device can be used to achieve symmetry and it can be made more interesting if the dancers move across each other's space (like invading each other's territory).

Complementary

This is where dancers perform movements that are similar but not exactly the same as each other. It is rather like an echo and can be easily achieved by changing levels or the line created by arms or legs. The **complementary** relationships could also be achieved by developing the action, for instance one dancer walks, another runs and a third leaps. The overall effect of complementary shapes and actions can be pleasing on the eye and is often used in ballet. See Photo B from *Overdrive* on page 16.

Contrast

Contrast is where dancers perform movements that have different dynamics or different shapes. You could also contrast action with stillness. In Photo **A** of *Rooster* by Christopher Bruce on page 94, each dancer is performing a **contrasting** movement.

> **Key terms**
> **Canon**: when movements overlap in time.
> **Complementary**: actions or shapes that are similar but not exactly the same.
> **Contrasting**: shapes or movements which are very different from each other.

> **Remember**
> Remember the difference between complementary (fills or completes) and complimentary (praise or a gift).

Accumulation

This is like follow the leader, where one dancer begins a series of movements and other dancers join in to all end at the same moment. It can add a sense of power as each dancer joins in turn. Christopher Bruce uses this effectively in the final section of *Ghost Dances*, where the dancer in the red dress performs a motif and the other villagers join in until they all dance in unison. At the beginning of *Front Line* by Henri Oguike the dancers enter one at a time and pick up the motif of the dancer in front of them so that they dance in unison. **Accumulation** can also be used in reverse, to 'drop off' dancers until there is only one left.

> **Key terms**
>
> **Accumulation**: when a dancer begins a series of movements and others join in until they all dance in unison.
>
> **Counterpoint**: when two or more dancers perform different phrases at the same time.

B *Counterpoint demonstrated through* Ghost Dances

Contact

This is where dancers lift, touch, lean on or support each other. Most choreographers use contact in some form and it is part of the vocabulary in most contemporary dance styles. Contact is an effective device for exploring and expressing emotional content and relationships between dancers, but it can also be used in an abstract way, with no specific meaning attached.

C *Faultline includes moments of contact*

Question and answer

This is where some of the group perform movements which are then contrasted or complemented by the rest of the group. This idea of a movement conversation can also be used effectively in a duo.

Foreground/background

This device is where one or more dancers perform the main material with the other dancers behaving rather like backing singers performing in the background with simpler material or repeated actions. Try this with some sequences that you are familiar with – you can have a lot of fun, especially when you change around the foreground and background dancers as part of the dance so that everyone has a go at being in the foreground.

Counterpoint

Counterpoint is when dancers perform individual movement sequences at the same time. Matthew Bourne uses counterpoint to reintroduce earlier movement material in the Wedding Party scene of *Nutcracker!* Counterpoint can be used effectively to build a climax or the end of a dance.

Activities

2. Practise a short dance that you know well (for instance the set study). Perform it in a group of 3–5 dancers, in unison.

3. Select two group relationships and include them in the dance. Perform the dance again. Can the rest of the class guess which dance relationships you have used?

4. Consider how these relationships add interest and expression to the dance.

Extension activity

Look at the Muybridge section in *Bird Song* for a clear example of a variety of relationships using four dancers.

Select another short section from a professional work you are studying and identify the different relationships used by the choreographer.

5.7 Group design

What are group formations?

These are the shapes and patterns created when a group of dancers performs. Typical designs include lines, circles, curves, V-shapes and squares. Dancers might be tightly clustered or scattered, and the arrangements they make could be **symmetric** or **asymmetric**. Dancers can also create structures in three dimensions (rather like sculptures). A good example can be seen in Nijinska's *Les Noces*, where the dancers create pyramid shapes. A line of dancers can be used to show power and solidarity, as the ghosts do in the opening section of *Ghost Dances*. On the other hand, a line of dancers can be fluid and ever-changing, as in the Snake section of *Bird Song*. A circle of dancers could express unity and harmony, but with one dancer in the centre the circle could symbolise something more menacing. Symmetric shapes and patterns can give the impression of balance and harmony; whereas asymmetric designs can have a more unbalanced and unpredictable feel. The dancers' focus, the actions and dynamic qualities they use will all affect the meaning or expression of group designs.

Why are they important?

As well as adding visual interest, group formations can help 'tell the story' and play an important part in structuring the dance by providing contrast and creating highlights and climaxes. The patterns created by five male dancers in the Utah Longhorn Ram section of *'Still Life' at the Penguin Café* are visually interesting; they also make the Ram soloist the star of the piece.

> **Objectives**
> Understand that group formations and numerical variation can enhance the dance idea.
>
> Make a more informed choice of solo or group choreography.

> **Key terms**
> **Symmetric**: the same on both sides or an equal balance of parts.
> **Asymmetric**: uneven.
> **Numerical variation**: how the number of dancers in a group is used.
> **Ensemble**: a group of dancers performing together.

What does numerical variation mean?

Numerical variation is how you use the number of dancers in the group in time, space and through action. Take five dancers and play with the sums:

- 1 + 1 + 1 + 1 + 1: dancers enter one at a time.
- 4 + 1: four dancers in unison with one dancer still.
- 2 + 3: contact work in duo and trio.
- 1 + 2 + 2: a sequence in canon started by one dancer.
- 5: all five dance in unison.

A *Images from nature make good stimuli for group formations*

Why is it important?

Like group formations, variations in number add interest, enhance the mood and meaning, and help structure the dance. In the Huajra section of *Ghost Dances*, Christopher Bruce uses a folk dance idea to create a lively dance in which three male and three female dancers perform as a six, as two trios and as three couples. In the first few minutes of *Overdrive*, Richard Alston creates a dynamic and restless effect by introducing his dancers in the following numerical order: 2, 2, 1, 3, 1, 6.

Odds or evens?

Odd numbers of dancers (such as threes and fives) create asymmetry and more opportunities for relationships. Trios achieve a dramatic effect in *Swansong* and *Faultline*, and for a more comic effect look at the Gobstopper dance in *Nutcracker!*

In contrast, the duos and a quartet in the Four Corners section of *Bird Song* create a more balanced and formal effect.

Solo, duo or group?

During the course you will have opportunities to work alone, in pairs and in different-sized groups. For your final assessment you have a choice of choreographing a solo, duo or group of up to five dancers. Give this careful consideration and weigh up the advantages and disadvantages of group size. It is important to choose the number of dancers that best suits your stimulus and movement idea, and remember that you do not have to perform in your own choreography.

A *The advantages and disadvantages of choreographing a dance for a solo and duo/group*

	Advantages	Disadvantages
Solo	Easier to rehearse (especially if you are the only dancer)	More material and development needed
Duo/group	Easier to step out of view as an outsider Less material needed and easier to develop More opportunities for spatial design	Difficult to get dancers together to rehearse You need good directing and interpersonal skills

Activities

1. In groups of four or five, in unison practise a short dance study that you know well.
2. Develop it to include the following in any order: line, circle, cluster, scatter, V-shape.
3. Evaluate the outcome – what did this add to the dance?
4. Develop what you have by manipulating the number of dancers in the group.

Activity

5. View an **ensemble** section from a professional work. Identify the different shapes and patterns formed by the dancers.

How do these enhance the dance idea?

Extension activity

Use the 'tag' solo you created (see page 49) and plan how to develop it for a duo (in your mind or on paper).

Work in threes – each person teaches their tag to the others but does not perform it themselves.

Find a way to combine the duos and find a role for the third dancer each time (for example still, off stage, performing a contrasting or complementary solo).

5.8 Structuring dances

What is meant by structure?

Structure is the framework on which a dance can be built. It would be difficult to write a short story without first having a framework, and in dance it is much the same. Devices such as motif and development, climax, contrast and repetition work with the framework to build the overall form of the dance. The close relationship shared by dance and music means that we borrow musical terms such as **binary**, **ternary** and **rondo**. Both dance and music happen over time, so repetition and variation of movements in dance and of melodies in music help to reinforce the ideas. Although most of the structural terms that follow originate from classical music, using these forms does not restrict you to a particular type of accompaniment or a particular style of dance.

Why is structure important?

Knowledge of structure will enhance your critical appreciation of dance. It will also help you as a choreographer, both in structuring your dance and in using music as accompaniment. When choreographing a short dance you have to be realistic and use a structure that is appropriate for your stimulus and dance ideas. You could explore the examples below as a class, but it would be quite a challenge to achieve some of them in a two- to three-minute choreography! What is vital, however, is for your choreography to have a good overall form with a clear beginning, middle and end.

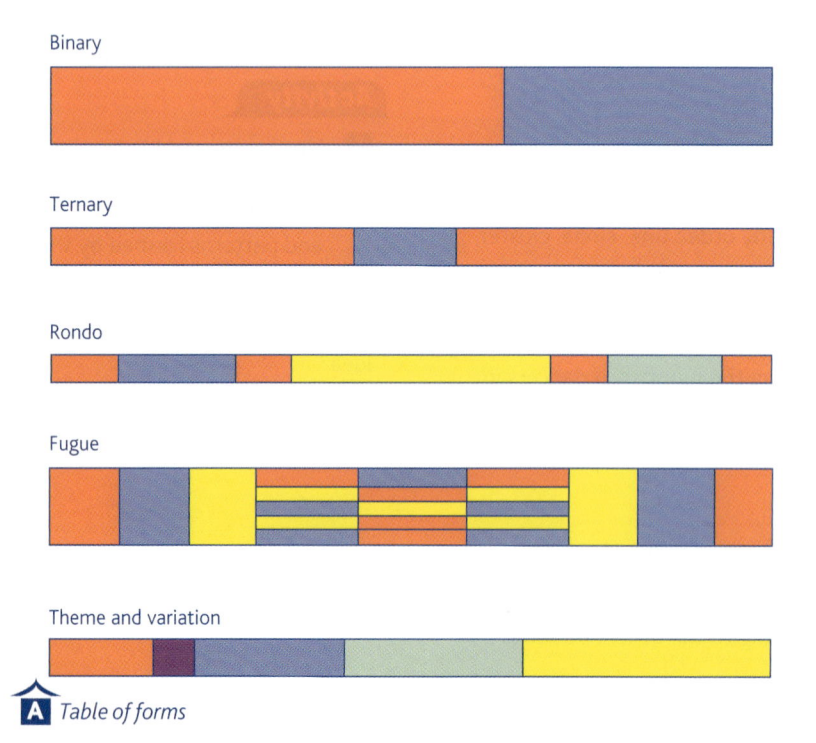

> **Objectives**
>
> Understand the importance of structure.
>
> Understand the links between structure and choreographic devices.
>
> Know about the different types of structure.

> **Key terms**
>
> **Binary**: a composition in two sections.
>
> **Ternary**: a composition in three sections, that is, A B A.
>
> **Rondo**: a musical form with an alternating and repeated section.
>
> **Cyclic**: something which has a circular feeling and which ultimately comes back to its own beginning.
>
> **Fugue**: interwoven phrases of movement or music.
>
> **Theme and variation**: where each section of a composition develops from the one before.
>
> **Episodic**: a choreography with several separate sections linked by a theme.

Binary

Ternary

Rondo

Fugue

Theme and variation

A Table of forms

Chapter 5 Creating dances

What structures can we use?

Binary

This is a dance in two sections (which do not need to be of equal length). The first section is established and the second section provides a contrast. Both sections would need something in common such as key actions or a clear theme. A dance about being trapped and free is an example of binary form.

Ternary

This is a dance in three sections, with sections one and three being similar and the middle section providing the contrast. The **cyclic** form helps to provide balance and a clear resolution (ending). You could use the ternary form for a dance based on the following: at work–tea-break–back to work.

Rondo

This form has a chorus that remains the same, but the melody of each verse is different to the one before. Mozart used the rondo form extensively, but a more recent musical example is *The Pink Panther* theme composed by Henry Mancini. You could use this to explore the idea of a spy on the lookout: on the prowl–on the lookout–falling into a trap–on the lookout.

Fugue

This is a complex and challenging form in which movement phrases from earlier in the dance are interwoven. It is often used by choreographers to build a climax towards the end of the dance. David Bintley uses **fugue** to create a climax. He reintroduces characters and their movement phrases from earlier scenes in a lively carnival scene in the Brazilian Woolly Monkey dance in *'Still Life' at the Penguin Café*.

Theme and variation

Theme and variation is a bit like Chinese whispers in that each section develops from the one before so that the end cannot be predicted. Although the end will be very different to the beginning, it should still contain some of the essence. The tag motif and development task (see page 49) is an example of theme and variation.

Narrative (or episodic)

This is where the theme or storyline unfolds a section at a time. *Nutcracker!* and *Romeo and Juliet* both have a narrative or **episodic** form. Christopher Bruce often builds his dramatic theme through short sections or episodes, usually with a different piece of music (or song) to accompany each section. *Ghost Dances*, *Swansong* and *'Still Life' at the Penguin Café* use the narrative form to explore central themes.

Activities

1. Find a piece of music in rondo form.
2. Create a simple group/class chorus and allocate each section to a different dancer.
3. Combine your ideas.
4. Find a myth or legend that inspires you to create a dance.
5. How would you divide the story (and dance) into different sections?

links

Refer to the section on choreographic devices (page 52).

AQA Examiner's tip

A dance with different sections needs to have effective transitions between each section. There should be a theme, idea or recognisable actions that hold the dance together.

5.9 The choreographic process

Guiding you through the process

> **Objectives**
>
> Learn about the process that you need to go through in order to create your dance.
>
> Learn about the things you need to consider in order to create a good choreography.

Flow chart:

- **Find something to dance about** → Refer back to pages 50–51 of this book for inspiration
- ↓
- **Research the idea and make a plan for your dance**
- ↓
- **Improvise and explore around potential movement material. Explore a suitable range of actions and dynamics to communicate the idea** → Create some original action content appropriate for the idea and then develop it using space, dynamics and relationships → Keep notes, draw diagrams, stick people and floor plans, etc
- ↓
- **Select and discard** → Create phrases and motifs and make choices – does your chosen material relate to the theme or idea?
- ↓
- **Develop using choreographic devices** → Consider spatial design; pathways, levels, directions, exits and entrances. Consider whether you use a variety of relationships for a group dance
  - → Think about how you have used a variety of different relationships in a group dance – can you use the differing relationships to help communicate the idea?
  - → Think about how you have used repetition with developments
- ↓
- **Structure** → Does the dance have shape – where are the contrasts, highlights and climax? Think about transitions
- ↓
- **Refine** → Think about your beginning and end – ask for some feedback from your teacher or your peers. Do the beginning and the end clearly relate to the theme or idea?
- → Get lots of feedback about your dance. Show it to people, video it, evaluate it and amend it

A *Creating your dance: from start to finish*

Activity

1 Using the choreographic plan you created for the Kandinsky picture on page 47:

a Research the idea and make a plan for your dance.

b Explore a suitable range of actions and dynamics to communicate the idea, and **improvise** and explore around potential movement material.

Key terms

Improvise: to explore and create movements without planning.

Evaluation checklist

Use this evaluation checklist to refine the progress of your work at any time:

1. How well have you used the stimulus?
2. Have you used original and varied action content?
3. Have you got contrasts in dynamics in your dance?
4. Is there variety in the use of relationships?
5. Have you thought about your use of space, levels, pathways, entrances and exits?
6. Have you included several motifs which encapsulate the dance idea?
7. What about repetition and development, contrast and variation, and unison/canon? Have you thought about where these might feature in your dance?
8. Have you thought about creating a good start and finish (offstage/onstage)?
9. Is there a climax in your dance, and are there highlights leading up to it?
10. Are there smooth and efficient transitions in the piece?
11. Is there a clear structure to your dance?
12. Have you thought about choreographing the use of focus into the dance?
13. Do you have moments of pause and stillness?
14. Have you chosen an appropriate accompaniment to enhance your dance idea?

AQA Examiner's tip

Check if your dance communicates your original idea. Video the finished piece and show it to family and friends, then talk to them to see if they are able to understand what your dance is about. What do you want your audience to feel?

Creating a dance is challenging. At times you will be completely stuck and unable to think of anything to do except discard everything and start all over again. There will be other times when you are on a roll and just want to keep going even though the lesson has ended. Remember, you are in control and the dance will not make itself up, so keep going and do not be beaten.

5.10 Choosing and using music

It is not essential to have music to accompany your dance, and sometimes a choreographer will choose to work without accompaniment, but at GCSE level, the majority of candidates like to use music to accompany their dance. It can be quite a challenge to find an appropriate piece of music, but if you choose wisely it can really enhance your dance idea. Conversely a bad choice can spoil it and in some cases detract from the choreography and from the message you were trying to get across.

Let us consider some of the reasons why we use music to accompany dance.

Objectives

Consider why we use music to accompany dance.

Consider how to make an appropriate choice of music for your own choreography.

links

Copyright-free music is downloadable from the web at www.freeplaymusic.com.

Hint

In a music shop or on a music website, look in the New Age, Electronic, Dance and Alternative categories for music with dynamic variety and interest.

Accompaniment adds:
- Rhythm/tempo
- Drama
- Cues
- Structure
- Mood/Atmosphere
- Climax
- Story
- Humour
- Style
- Dynamics
- Sense of place
- Phrasing
- Interest

A *What does music add to a dance?*

Did you know ??????

- Joining more than two pieces of music usually results in lack of unity.
- Odd cuts or complete changes of music within a dance suggest a lack of choreographic understanding.
- Poor musical editing can spoil a dance.

Look at Diagram **A**. See what particular areas you want the music to serve for your choreography and then get searching. For example, do you want the music to add mood and atmosphere to your dance? Are you hoping it will add humour? It is important to establish how you think your choice of music will help you to communicate the dance idea, because that will make it easier for you to narrow down your choice. The internet is a good place to start, and on some websites you can listen to snippets of music before you buy an entire track. You can, of course, edit one or two tracks and splice them together, but you must be mindful of the fact that the editing of music could infringe copyright law.

Choosing your aural setting

When choosing your aural setting:

- Take the trouble to find a suitable piece of music; do not just use silence because you cannot be bothered to find something more suitable.
- Make sure there are connections between the accompaniment and your theme/idea.
- Choose music with **dynamic variation** and contrast – or edit pieces to include them – because it makes choreographing highlights/climax easier.
- Experiment with the use of a variety of different accompaniments, including spoken word, natural sound and found sounds.
- Do not use songs with lyrics that are about something completely different to the theme of your choreography.
- Avoid using popular chart music with limited dynamic variation, and similarly music that has an even pace throughout, because you will find it very difficult to create dynamic interest in the dance.
- Avoid using music which has to be manually faded at the end of the dance because this almost always results in a weak ending to the choreography.
- Make sure you know and can cite the title(s) of tracks used and the name of the composer/artist.

Finding the right piece of music for your choreography is certainly a challenge, but since you can gain some vital extra marks for making an appropriate choice, it is worth spending time to find what you really want. Talk to your dance teacher who will probably have lots of music for you to listen to, and do not be afraid to try several very different tracks to perform the same dance. Oddly enough you can make any dance fit to any piece of music if you change the dynamics.

> **Key terms**
>
> **Dynamic variation**: variety in the quality or the 'how' of the movement, for example the use of different kinds of speed, energy and flow in a dance.

> **AQA Examiner's tip**
>
> You will be awarded marks in the choreography task for your choice of aural setting. Your teacher and moderator will assess you on your appropriate choice of accompaniment to complement the artistic intention of your work.

> **Remember**
>
> You could create a recording or soundscape of natural sounds to accompany your work. *Cross Channel* by Lea Anderson uses everyday sounds to accompany the dance.

> **Activity**
>
> Try out a dance that you have created, or that you know well, to at least three different types of accompaniment that you would not normally think of using. Evaluate the effect of each.

5.11 The choreography tasks

There are two separate choreographic tasks in the AQA GCSE Dance exam and they make up Unit 4. They are both assessed by your teacher who will decide the exact time in your course when this will happen. You will almost certainly work on one piece before the other, and this will help you to develop your choreographic skills.

> **Objectives**
>
> Learn about the two tasks that make up the choreography unit in the AQA GCSE Dance examination.

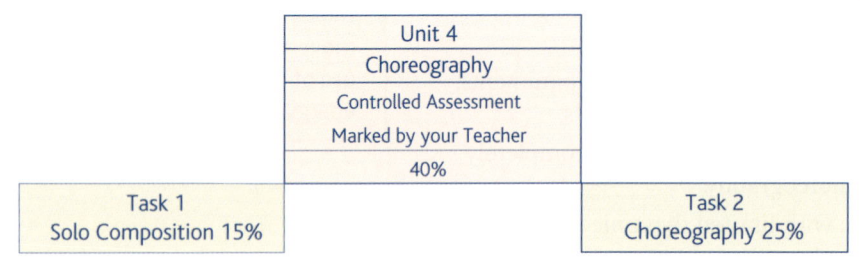

	Unit 4 Choreography Controlled Assessment Marked by your Teacher 40%	
Task 1 Solo Composition 15%		Task 2 Choreography 25%

A *The two choreography tasks*

Task 1: solo composition

With the help of your teacher you will select three motifs from a professional work and develop them into a short solo dance with clear form and structure. Your finished dance will be between 60 and 90 seconds long.

Your teacher will be marking you on:

- the ways in which you analyse, evaluate and develop your work to improve it during the working process and in the finished product
- evidence of your having developed the action, space and dynamic content of your original motifs in an imaginative way
- successful linking and integration of the motifs into your composition
- successful use of choreographic devices and principles (see pages 56–57).

It is likely that you will want to perform your own work in this task, but the quality of your performance is not awarded any specific marks.

What makes a good solo composition?

Here is AQA's definition of a very good solo composition:

The candidate shows an inspired, creative and original response in developing the material and integrating all three motifs. The structure of the piece is highly appropriate and the use of choreographic devices very effective. The whole piece has unity. The candidate demonstrates highly developed analytical and evaluative skills to bring about improvement during the realisation of the task.

Task 2: solo/group choreography

You will choose a starting point or stimulus from the following:

- words, a poem or piece of text (can include instructions, etc.)
- a photograph or a piece of 2D or 3D art
- a prop, **accessory** or piece of fabric
- a feature of the natural world
- a piece of music composed before 1970
- an everyday activity; a topical or historical event.

You will then choreograph a solo or group dance. If you choose to create a solo it needs to be between one-and-a-half and two minutes long. A group dance must be between two-and-a-half and three minutes long and be created for two, three, four or a maximum of five dancers. You decide if you want to be in your own dance or if you want to choreograph it for someone else to perform. As in Task 1, the quality of the performance is not awarded any specific marks.

The important thing to remember is that the dance you choreograph must be all your own work, although you will obviously get feedback from other people and from your dancers on how things are progressing during the rehearsal process. You will also have to choose your own accompaniment for your dance as you will be awarded marks for making an appropriate choice in this area.

On the day of your assessment your teacher will be looking to see how well you have achieved the following:

- creative and imaginative response to your stimulus/starting point
- appropriate and imaginative choice of action content
- use of a variety of dynamics
- use of space with interest and variety
- use of different group relationships where appropriate
- overall form and structure of your dance
- use of choreographic devices and principles
- appropriate choice of accompaniment
- successful communication of the dance idea.

> **Key terms**
> **Accessory:** an additional item of costume, for example gloves.

> **AQA Examiner's tip**
> These two choreography tasks carry a lot of marks. They are worth 40 per cent of the whole of your GCSE.

> **Remember**
> This is a really exciting part of the GCSE course, where you will have the opportunity to show just how imaginative and creative you can be.

Chapter summary

In this chapter you have learnt:

In this chapter you have learnt how to choose a stimulus for choreography and discovered why it is important to make a really good choice. You have considered a range of different kinds of stimuli and learned how to focus that idea into something which will work for a piece of choreography. You have looked at ways of planning a dance and the importance of thinking your idea through and imagining what your dance will look like before you start work on creating the movement material.

You have considered a range of techniques and devices that you can use to add interest and depth to your work and you have looked at different ways in which you can manipulate your dancers in a group dance and your material in a solo. You have thought about the structure of your dance and you now have a really good idea of the processes that you need to go through in order to achieve a sound piece of choreography. Finally you have looked at the requirements for both choreography tasks and you now know what you need to do in order to gain good marks in your assessments.

Revision quiz

1. Name three different types of stimuli.
2. What is a motif?
3. Name three ways in which you can develop a motif.
4. Name two choreographic approaches.
5. Explain what is meant by a highlight in a dance.
6. What is canon?
7. Explain what is meant by question and answer in dance.
8. Why is it important to use a variety of relationships in a group dance?
9. Name one type of structuring device and explain what it does.
10. How many tasks make up Unit 4, Choreography?

6 Performing dances

In this chapter you will learn about:

- the physical and expressive skills that you will need to develop in order to improve your performing skills
- different approaches that you can use when rehearsing your work
- what you will do in the two performance units for the examination
- how you will be assessed in the tasks.

Performing for an audience

Performing in front of an audience is one of the most exciting aspects of being a dancer. It is a time when you hope that everything you have learnt comes together. You push yourself to your limits to try to achieve your best whilst experiencing a whole range of emotions from 'absolutely terrified' to 'really proud' in practically the same breath!

By learning about the many different ways in which you can improve your performance ability you will discover that you can perform with even greater confidence and enjoyment.

Discover what makes a good performance

Of course, performing well is about so much more than just learning the steps and then going over and over them again until you can do the dance without having to think about what comes next. This is really only the very first stage of perfecting a performance. This chapter explains what makes a good performance and suggests some of the ways that you can develop these skills for yourself. In a professional company there will probably be a rehearsal director who helps the dancers by focusing their rehearsals on a particular feature or target. All rehearsals need to have a focus, so use the information in this chapter to help you target every single rehearsal you do. That way you will get the most benefit from them.

A Practice makes perfect

6.1 Technical skills in performing

Why do we need good technique?

One of the first things we notice when we see professional dancers performing on stage is how technically strong they are. This is hardly surprising given that most of them will have spent several hours each day, probably for many years, training their bodies to try and reach perfection in their dance technique. Good technique underpins everything we do in dance. It makes the work look easy to an audience and helps to develop our physical facility. So what kinds of things do professional dancers do in their daily classes and how does this relate to what you need to work on in your technical sessions?

How professional dancers improve their technical skill

The mind map in Diagram **A** shows you some of the things the professional dancer will be working on in class to improve his or her technical ability. This is then carried over into rehearsals for performances. These are exactly the same things that you need to be working on in your own classes.

Objectives

Learn about technical performing skills.

A Technical performing skills

Mind map of Technical performing skills: Good posture, Determination, Concentration, Relationship, Good alignment, Control, Stamina, Coordination, Action, Balance, Strength, Flexibility, Mobility, Dynamics, Space, Focus, Confidence.

Activity

1. Choose five of the skills from the mind map in Diagram **A** and identify how you might work to improve these in a technique class. You could apply your thinking to a particular dance or think about it generally. For example:
   a. action – better execution of movements (jump higher, spin faster)
   b. space – think about and plot out on paper how you place the dance in the space and where you perform certain parts of the work.

If you are not sure what some of the words in the mind map mean you may need to discuss them with your teacher or look in the glossary of this book.

Remember

Before you commence a technique class, you must complete a warm-up. See Chapter 3, Safe dance practice, pages 24–25.

How to improve your technical skill

Building good **technical skill** is vital to ensuring a good performance. Work hard in class to try and improve your technical skill so that you can put it into practice when you are performing in your group dance and your set dance and remember, good technique is developed through a focused mind. You will not improve your technical ability if you do not concentrate 100 per cent in every class. Nor will you improve if you do not really want to! Sometimes our minds and our bodies get lazy and there are bound to be times when you really do not feel like pushing yourself in class, but this is precisely the time when you will have to be very determined and self-motivated if you want to improve.

Key terms

Technical skill: the ability to control what the body does.

Hint

Get a friend to take some photographs of you performing. Analyse the photographs and identify some areas to work on in order to improve your own technical skill.

B *These dancers are demonstrating technical skill*

Look at the photograph of two dancers performing (Photo **B**). It was taken in the middle of a live performance and although it is only a frozen moment, we can see evidence of each dancer's technical skill.

Activity

2 Look at the mind map in Diagram **A**. Taking each of the skills in turn, see if you can identify their presence in the photo of the two dancers. Are there any skills that are difficult to identify in a photograph? Are there any skills that these dancers could improve?

Did you know ???????

If you think about being a piece of elastic and creating long lines in your movement, it helps you stretch right to the ends of your toes and fingers, and makes your work look much better. This is called extension.

6.2 Expressive skill in performance

What makes a dance performance special?

Think about one of the professional works that you have seen. All of the dancers in it are great technicians, but is there something more than that? What is it that makes one dancer stand out from another even though they might both be doing exactly the same thing? What is it that makes us want to watch a particular dancer and causes us to be drawn to watch them? Some might call it the 'X factor', but in dance we call it expression or artistry.

> **Objectives**
> Learn about the importance of using expression when performing dances.

What are expressive skills?

Expressive skills are the things that give a performance its own energy, that make it engaging to watch and make you respond to it emotionally. A performance can be technically stunning, but without expression or artistry it would be lacking something really crucial. The mind map in Diagram **A** shows the artistic or expressive skills that we consider important in a performance.

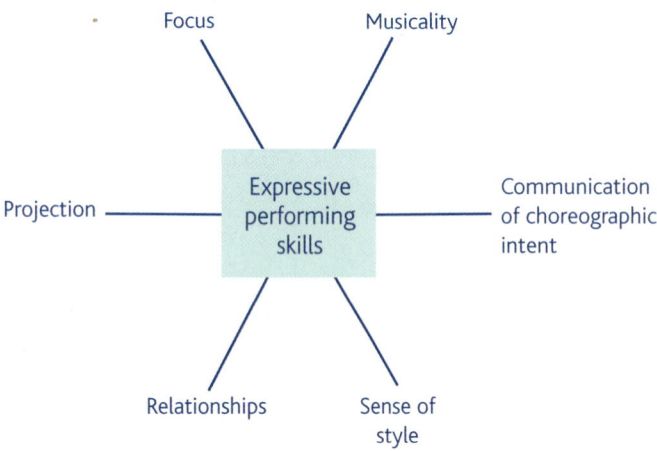

```
         Focus         Musicality
            \           /
             \         /
   Projection — Expressive — Communication
             /  performing  \  of choreographic
            /     skills     \      intent
           /                   \
      Relationships         Sense of
                             style
```

A *Expressive performing skills*

How do expressive skills affect a performance?

- Focus: this is about the dancer's sightline and how and where the dancer looks.
- Projection: this is about the energy and power of the performance and the way in which it communicates with and draws in the audience.
- Sense of style: this is about the dancer trying to emulate the distinctive actions and qualities of the dance.
- **Musicality**: this is all about communicating an inner feeling for or sensitivity to the accompaniment.
- Communication of choreographic intent: this is about the dancer understanding and empathising with the mood or meaning of the dance and communicating that feeling to the audience.

> **Key terms**
> **Musicality**: the ability to pick out the unique qualities of the accompaniment and make them evident through the performance.

These skills are very difficult to acquire and you will need to work on developing them throughout your course if you are going to lift your performance work into the top mark categories. The important thing to remember is that the skills provide the key to making the difference between just going through the motions of **doing** a dance and really **performing** it. If you can develop these skills, your audience will appreciate your performance much more, because they will feel like they are sharing the joy of the performance with you.

Activities

1. Look at a short section from a professional work. With a partner, try to identify places where some of the expressive skills identified above are being demonstrated and talk through how the dancer communicates those skills.

2. What expressive skills can you see in use in Photo **B**? Do you think the dancers in this duet are working expressively? Give reasons to support your answer.

AQA Examiner's tip

You will need to develop your technical and expressive skills in performance if you want to achieve high marks.

B *Work on developing your expressive skills throughout the course*

6.3 Achieving high-quality performance

How to practise effectively

You will probably have a very clear idea of what you want to look like when you are doing your performance, but knowing how to achieve it can be much more difficult. Obviously you will have to practise a dance to learn the content and then, when you know it, you will need to work on improving your expressive skills. But if all you do is to keep going over the same thing again and again, it will soon get boring, and you may even be reinforcing mistakes or errors!

Rehearsal

What things can you do to vary your rehearsal, to make it more interesting and to be sure that you are rehearsing accurately? Here are a few suggestions. You may be able to think up some even more creative ideas for making your rehearsal more effective.

- Buddying up with a partner.
- Watching your classmates and providing collective whole-class feedback.
- Watching others performing and analysing the good things that you want to emulate in your own work.
- Mental rehearsal – where you visualise your performance in your head without even moving off the spot (it often helps to close your eyes whilst you do this). This helps your movement memory.
- Using mirrors for personal feedback.
- Setting yourself targets to work towards.
- Getting feedback from a teacher.
- Asking for help with movements or aspects that you find difficult.
- Rehearsing in front of an audience as often as possible – an audience can be just one or two people.
- Asking someone to record your performance on video so that you can evaluate your own work.
- Designing a rehearsal plan or schedule of what aspects of good performance you are going to work on next.
- Being very clear about (and being able to describe) the action and the spatial and dynamic content of the dance you are performing.

You can improve your work in performance by rehearsing and practising, but it is important to also get lots of feedback so that you can set yourself targets to work towards.

> **Objectives**
> Think about the different ways you can rehearse your work to make it better.

> **Did you know ??????**
> Athletes use mental rehearsal immediately before a race and they imagine themselves achieving their goals. This often helps them perform better. Professional dancers use the same technique before they go on stage. They imagine themselves giving a faultless performance and this often helps them do just that; try this yourself before you perform.

Activities

1. Imagine you are going to rehearse your set dance for half an hour every day during one school week. Draw up a rehearsal schedule making sure you include details of the specific technical and expressive skills that you plan to work on in each session. Hopefully by the time you get to the end of the week you will have worked on a range of skills. Try to incorporate more than one way of working so it

Chapter 6 Performing dances

does not get boring. Table **A** is a sample rehearsal schedule that has been started for you.

2. Look at the dancers rehearsing in Photo **B**. If you were leading this group, what advice would you give to the dancers to help them improve their performances?

A *Partially completed rehearsal schedule*

Session	Work on	Method	Technical skills to focus on	Expressive skills to focus on
Monday	First six bars of set dance	Mental rehearsal Repetition Buddy-up	Alignment Balance Use of space	Projection
Tuesday				
Wednesday				
Thursday				
Friday				

B *Watch your classmates rehearse and give feedback on their performance*

6.4 Performance in a duo/group dance – Unit 3

What you will do in this unit

The dance you will perform for Unit 3 will have links with a professional work chosen for you by your teacher. The dance will have two, three, four or five dancers in it. The total length of the finished piece must be between three and three-and-a-half minutes, and you will be on stage performing for at least two minutes of that time.

> **Objectives**
>
> Learn about the requirements of Unit 3 – Performance in a duo/group dance.

Who will choreograph the dance?

It is possible that your teacher or maybe even a dance artist will make up the complete piece, but it is also possible that you will be asked to give some ideas or even choreograph small sections yourself. The important thing to remember is that the dance must be designed to allow you plenty of opportunity to demonstrate your skill in the aspects that you are going to be marked on, so your teacher will keep these in mind when they create the dance. The important thing to remember is that although you are working as a group, you will all be marked for your own individual and personal contribution to the piece.

What you will be assessed on

The AQA GCSE Dance specification describes very good performance as follows:

The candidate demonstrates excellent technical ability and accurate execution of action, dynamic and spatial content in relation to the demands of the choreography. There is sensitive interpretation of the mood and meaning of the dance and this is communicated throughout the performance. The candidate is highly sensitive to other performers and produces a completely engaging performance which communicates a real sense of performance energy to the audience. All aspects of safe practice are evidenced and applied appropriately.

Here is a list of the six aspects that you will be assessed on in your performance:

1. Your technical ability (see pages 70–71).
2. How accurately you perform the choreographed action, dynamic and spatial content of the dance.
3. How well you interpret and communicate the mood or meaning of the dance.
4. The way in which you demonstrate sensitivity to and an awareness of other dancers (see Chapter 3, Safe dance practice, pages 26–27).
5. How well you demonstrate your own safe practice as a performer in carrying out movements safely, and through the way in which you present yourself personally for the performance (see Chapter 3, Safe dance practice, pages 28–29).
6. Your overall sense of expression within the performance (see page 72).

Chapter 6 Performing dances 77

You will see that most of the marks are about you as an individual, but point 4 is about you working with other dancers. This is very important because the way that you interact with other dancers is critical to the success of this performance. For example, if you are not in the right place at the right time in the dance you will almost certainly affect the performance of another dancer. It is therefore very important for you to get together with the other members of your group to discuss ways of improving all of the things that affect you collectively as a group. Here are some examples of the kinds of things you might want to discuss and focus on in your rehearsals:

- Achieving perfect unison where applicable.
- Using the space well and effectively.
- Collective use of focus.
- Alignment.

What other things can you think of that are important to the overall effectiveness of your group dance?

You now know what is expected of you in this unit. When you are rehearsing your piece, it is a good idea to keep checking your own performance against the marking criteria so that you can work on improving.

> **AQA Examiner's tip**
> Get someone to video you in your finished group dance and then you can watch and check your own contribution to the piece against the marking criteria above.

> **links**
> See the rehearsal tips on pages 74–75 to find different ways of monitoring and improving your performance.

> **Remember**
> You will lose marks if you do anything to detract from your performance, such as talking, adjusting your clothing or flicking your hair back.

> **Hint**
> Always try to perform with a sense of energy and commitment. Make sure you are 'performing' the dance, not just 'doing it'.

> **Did you know ??????**
> This unit is worth 20 per cent of your total GCSE marks.

A *Young dancers performing with a strong sense of focus*

6.5 Solo set dance – Unit 2

What you will perform

Two dances have been specially created by professional choreographers for this unit and you will perform one of them for assessment. Your teacher will decide if you are going to learn just one or both of them during your course.

The dances are approximately one minute long. You will need to learn the action, dynamic and spatial content accurately, exactly as the choreographer intended, but you will have the opportunity of really showing your performing skills to the full through the way you interpret the expressive elements of the dance.

Who will mark your work?

This performance will be marked by an examiner, so at some point in your course your teacher will let you know that you are going to be filmed on video performing the dance for the very last time. The video recording will then be sent away to an examiner who will assess your work.

What you will be marked on

There are six aspects that you will be assessed on in your performance, and not surprisingly they are very similar to the aspects you will be assessed on in the duo/group performance. They are:

1. Your technical ability.
2. How accurately you perform the choreographed action, dynamic and spatial content of the dance.
3. Your overall sense of performance.
4. Your ability to emulate the style and mood of the original choreography.
5. How well you demonstrate your own safe practice as a performer in carrying out movements safely, and through the way in which you present yourself personally for the performance.
6. The way you interpret the dynamic and expressive qualities of the dance.

> **Objectives**
> Learn about the requirements of Unit 2 – Performance in a set dance.

> **Hint**
> Ask your teacher for a copy of the simple counting grid from the set dance notes. If you chant the words on the grid out loud or in your head, it will help you to learn the order of the actions in the study.

What makes a good performance of the solo set dance?

Here is AQA's description of a very good solo set dance:

'The candidate demonstrates excellent technical ability and accurate execution of action and spatial requirements. There is sensitive interpretation of the dynamic and expressive qualities throughout and sensitive interpretation of the style and mood of the set dance. The candidate produces a completely engaging performance which communicates a real sense of performance energy to the audience. All aspects of safe practice are evidenced and applied appropriately.'

How can you improve your performance?

Performing someone else's choreography can be challenging especially if it is in a style you are not used to working with. Make sure you watch the DVD of professional dancers performing the dance and then try to work out what things make the dance unique and give it its own personality or character. These are what we call the characteristic features. Once you have done this your teacher will be able to tell you what the choreographer has identified as being important to their particular choreography. It is really important for you to know these characteristic features because if you understand what the choreographer was trying to do when they made up the dance, it will be much easier for you to emulate the style and mood of the original choreography.

Remember this dance has been choreographed by a professional choreographer and you are learning their work just like you would if you belonged to a professional company. Your job is to carry out the choreographer's wishes, not to amend or alter the work to make it easier or because you do not like a particular part. To summarise, you must perform the action and spatial content completely accurately as the choreographer intended and with the correct timing, but you do have the chance to 'make it your own' through the way in which you apply expressive skills such as musicality and projection.

Activity

Work with a partner to watch each others' performance of the solo dance and help each other to identify moments that need work.

links

See the rehearsal techniques on pages 74–75 to discover different ways of monitoring and improving your performance.

Chapter summary

In this chapter you have learnt:

In this chapter you have learnt about the range of technical and expressive skills that go together to make a good performance. You should now understand what you need to do and what you will be assessed on in your duo/group performance and you have looked at the criteria the examiner will use to mark you in your performance of the set dance. Most importantly you now know how to improve your performance by using a variety of different rehearsal techniques.

Revision quiz

1. What is meant by technical skill?
2. Identify three technical skills.
3. What is meant by expressive skill?
4. Identify three expressive skills.
5. What is the maximum number of dancers that are allowed to perform in the duo/group performance?
6. What aspects of safe dance practice will you be assessed on in the set dance?
7. How might you use a video recording of yourself performing to improve your work?
8. What is meant by the term 'mental rehearsal'?

Diagram **A** is the start of a mind map to identify what you can do to improve your performance. How many more branches can you add?

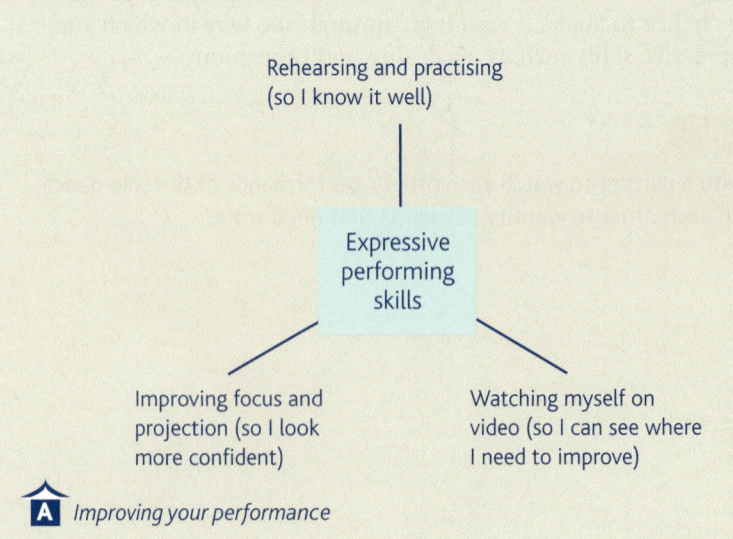

- Rehearsing and practising (so I know it well)
- Expressive performing skills
  - Improving focus and projection (so I look more confident)
  - Watching myself on video (so I can see where I need to improve)

A Improving your performance

7 Aspects of production

In this chapter you will learn about:
- different types of physical settings, aural settings and costumes
- how physical settings, aural settings and costumes add importance to a dance work.

Key terms
Proscenium: the arch or opening which separates a stage from the auditorium.

In-the-round: a performing area with the audience seated on all sides.

Site-specific: dances that are designed for non-theatre spaces, for example for a museum, the beach, etc.

Props: portable objects that are used in a dance, for example a suitcase or newspaper.

AQA Examiner's tip
You will be asked questions about the relationship between choreography, performance and production in your written examination, so making notes when you watch a dance performance on video/DVD or see a live dance performance will help you to prepare for the exam.

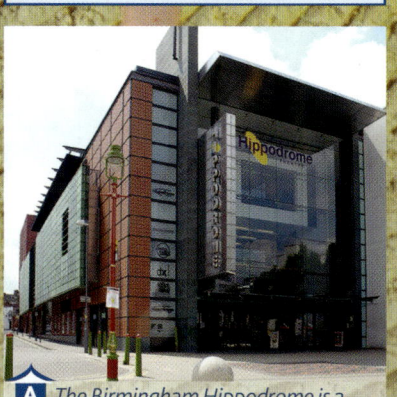

A *The Birmingham Hippodrome is a major professional dance venue in the UK*

Identifying the different features of dance works

Much of the GCSE Dance exam concentrates on preparing you for performing and choreographing dances, but the course also requires you to demonstrate your ability to appreciate and critique dance.

The effectiveness of the movement is only one aspect that you need to consider when evaluating a dance work. For Unit 1 you will be expected to understand the relationship between choreography, performance and production, including aural and physical settings, costume and dance for camera.

Physical setting
- The performance space or staging (for example proscenium, in-the-round, site-specific, naturalistic, symbolic, abstract).
- Set design (for example lighting, props, projection features: colour, material, texture, decoration, shape and levels).
- The relationship between the physical setting and dance content.

Aural setting
- Different types of accompaniment (for example song, spoken word, natural sound, and music from different times and places).
- The features of accompaniment (for example tone, texture, rhythm, dynamics, style, structure).
- The relationship between music and dance.

Costume
- What dancers wear when they perform and they can be realistic or abstract. Features include colour, texture, flow, shape, weight, decoration, line accessories, footwear, masks and make-up.
- The relationship between costume and dance content.

Dance for camera
The following things should be considered:
- Placement, angle, distance/proximity.
- Special effects.
- The relationship between the camera and the dance content.

Starter activity
1. Think about any dance work you have seen.
2. List as many features of the set and costume as you can.
3. Try to remember the details.

7.1 Physical setting

Dances are performed in many different environments that can range from inside a theatre to outside on a beach for example. Choreographers use many features to enhance the set design such as lighting, props and projections. These features can often make the meaning of a dance work clear to an audience as well as creating a visual impact.

Set design

Set designs vary enormously. The set might be a bare stage with coloured lighting such as in *Overdrive*. Or it may include **backdrops** such as in *'Still Life' at the Penguin Café*, where the habitat of each animal is shown on a backdrop. Some sets look like real places, complete with pieces of furniture such as the armchair that is used by Juliet during the nursery scene in *Romeo and Juliet* by Kenneth MacMillan. A set within *Perfect* by Kevin Finnan and Motionhouse has sand on the floor of the stage; the dancers play with the sand and pass it to each other as well as dancing through it. The inclusion of such a feature is the choreographer's choice. It is the choreographer who decides what might increase an audience's understanding of a dance work.

> **Objectives**
>
> Learn about different types of physical settings.
>
> Understand how physical setting can contribute to dance works.

> **Key terms**
>
> **Backdrops**: walls or drapes at the back of the stage usually painted with a decorative scene, picture or design.

A *The nursery scene in* Romeo and Juliet

Chapter 7   Aspects of production   83

Lighting

Lighting can be a very important feature of a dance work. Some choreographers use lights to flood the stage with colour, as can be seen in *Overdrive* by Richard Alston. Other choreographers, such as Henri Oguike (*Front Line*) and Russell Maliphant (*Shift*), use lighting as the set design, cleverly hiding, sculpting or highlighting body parts or casting shadows to make one dancer appear as several dancers.

Lighting can also be used to highlight key moments or climaxes in dance works. For example, at the end of each section of *Ghost Dances*, a bright yellow/green light appears and this, along with the stillness of the dancers and the silence of the accompaniment, tells the audience that a life has been taken. Lighting can also act as a symbol in a dance work. In *Swansong*, the diagonal white light appearing from upstage left during the prisoner's solo dances and in the final section could suggest freedom, heaven and so on. You can see this clearly in Photo **B**. These and other uses of lighting such as the position, placement, direction and intensity can help the audience understand the meaning of a dance work.

Activity

1. Draw a lighting design for one of the pieces of dance that you have created during this course.
   a. Think about the colours you would choose to help make the idea for the dance clear to an audience.
   b. Where would you place lights? How bright would they be? Would you use spotlights?
   c. Give reasons for your choices.

B *Lighting helps to communicate the meaning of a dance to the audience*

Projection

Projected images can be used with great effect in dance works. Look at the film of soprano Patricia Rozario projected onto the wall in *Faultline*. The singer is given importance in the performance by being seen in the work as she is projected onto the backdrop. Or look at Section 4a or Section 1 (Snake) in *Bird Song* by Siobhan Davies where a series of pulsating dots is projected onto the dance floor. The flickering is caused by placing a grid over a film of birds flying and it supports Davies' idea breaking movement into fragmented phrases. These projections can help an audience to understand the choreographer's idea or intention.

> **Activity**
>
> 2 You are creating a dance based on the theme of travel. What types of projections could you use to help make this idea clear to an audience?

Props

The use of props can add meaning to a dance as well as being used for decoration. Props are usually items that can be carried or moved on stage rather than being fixed. Many props are used in Matthew Bourne's *Nutcracker!* For example, skipping ropes are used by the orphans in Act 1.

C *The orphans from* Nutcracker!

The canes used by the guards in *Swansong* are props that enhance movement. The guards lean on the canes and leap over them to enhance the theme of the dance. They also use the canes to beat the prisoner.

The chair in *Swansong* is also a prop, although its use in the dance is so important that Christopher Bruce, the choreographer, considered the chair to be part of the set. The chair has many uses in *Swansong*. It represents a shield, a weapon, a safe haven, burden, prison bars and shackles. The prisoner's relationship to the chair changes throughout the dance, giving the audience an idea of his state of mind as the dance progresses.

D *A selection of costume and props that can be incorporated into dance*

Activities

3 Using some of the ideas mentioned for *Swan Song*, choreograph a duet that features a chair.

4 Can you think of any other uses for the chair?

7.2 The use of features in physical settings

The features of physical settings can add meaning to a dance work. The use of colour, texture, shape and size of features within a set can have huge importance.

Objectives

Learn about the different features of physical settings.

Understand how different features of physical settings can contribute to dance works.

Colour

The colours used in a set can help to create an atmosphere or mood for the dance. In *Nutcracker!* by Matthew Bourne the black and white colours of the backdrop and floor tell the audience that the orphanage is not a happy place and that the orphans are not very well treated. When the colours change in the skating scene of Act 2 and there is blue sky with a white pillow, we then think either that the mood is happier or that Clara is having a dream.

Texture

The texture of the set creates a visual impact for a dance work. In *Perfect* by Kevin Finnan and Motionhouse, there is sand covering the floor of the stage. This is used by the dancers, who pass the sand through their fingers and dance through it. The set designer of *Perfect*, Simon Dormon, says: 'It has always been interesting working with dancers on designing objects with movement in mind ... Function usually becomes more important as the physical relationship is often intense between dancer and surface.'

Decoration

Decoration, or lack of it, can help the audience gain a better understanding of the choreographer's intention. In *'Still Life' at the Penguin Café* by David Bintley, the backdrop changes for each animal featured in the dance. In the Texan kangaroo rat section, there is a backdrop of a giant green cactus with a yellow and sand-coloured background, telling the audience that the rat lives in a desert environment. The size of the cactus suggests that the rat is very small. There are tables and chairs on either side of the stage, where the dancers sit and appear to be entertained by the other dancers.

Shape

Features such as the giant, pink, heart-shaped flower garland that frames Princess Sugar and the Nutcracker in Act 2 of *Nutcracker!* by Matthew Bourne help the narrative of the story. We know that the two dancers are in love and are about to get married.

Chapter 7 Aspects of production 87

Levels

The set can be used to create levels for the dancers to sit, lie or dance on, for example low (floor), medium (normal standing height) and high (in the air). In *Ghost Dances* by Christopher Bruce there are some rocks in front of the backdrop. The ghost characters stand on them at the beginning and end of the dance and hide behind them during moments of the dance, appearing from behind them to take the lives of the dancers. The dancers sit on them during some of the sections of the work. These levels can add some depth and height to the dance.

A *The heart scene from Matthew Bourne's* Nutcracker!

Activity

1. Look at the photograph of *Swansong* on page 17.
    a. The choreographer has the dancers using different levels. How has he done this?
    b. What does this use of different levels tell us about the relationship between the dancers?

7.3 The performing space

Types of performing space

Proscenium

Dance is performed in many different spaces which can be of varying sizes. Traditionally dance was performed on a proscenium stage and this is often used today in classical ballet. These traditional stages are placed at one end of the auditorium so that the audience all face the same direction. There are usually wings on either side of the stage where dancers enter and exit the stage.

> **Objectives**
>
> Learn about different types of performing space.
>
> Understand how different performing spaces can contribute to dance works.

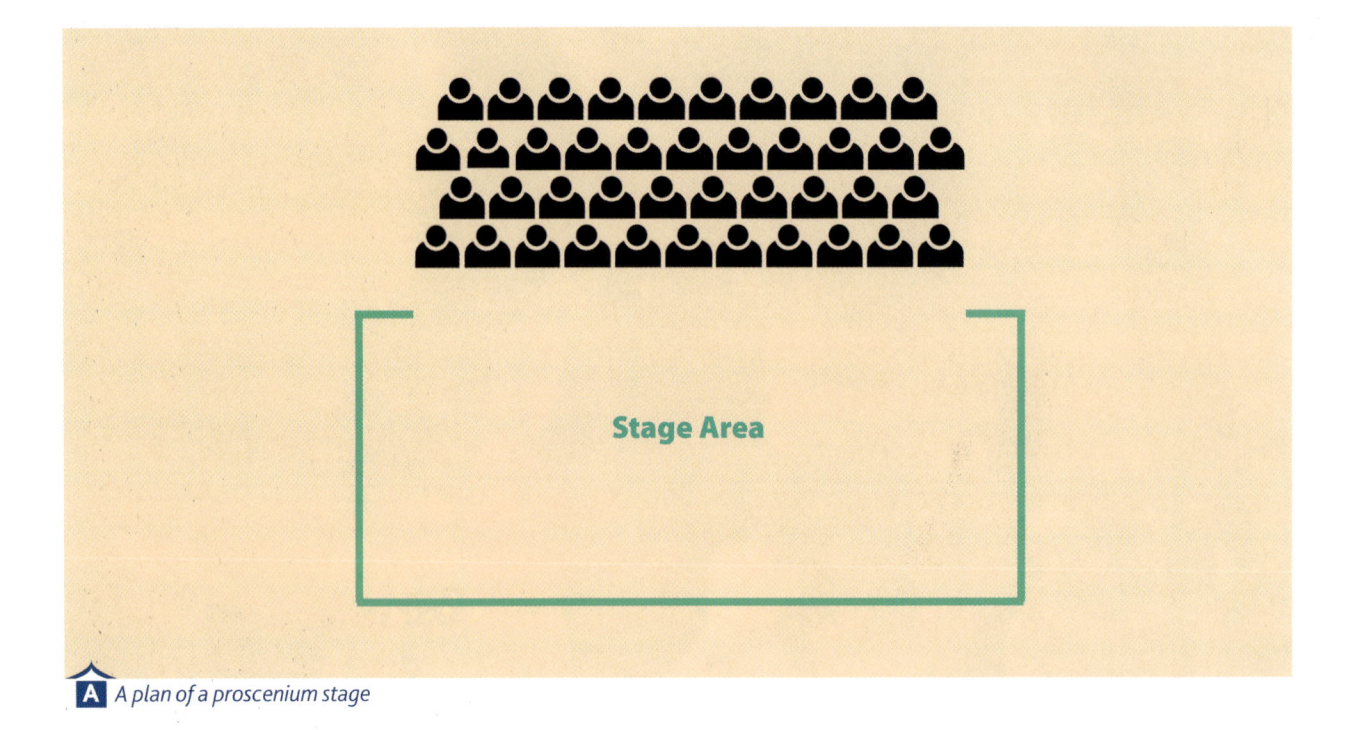

A A plan of a proscenium stage

Cyclorama

A **cyclorama** can be used to help create a performing space. In such spaces a backdrop is often used. The backdrop can be plain black or white in order for the lighting to create a wash of colour.

Alternatively, the backdrop can have an image of where the dance is set. For example, in *Ghost Dances* by Christopher Bruce, the backdrop has a landscape painted on it, suggesting that the dance is set within a cave, and the audience can see the landscape outside. A dance work can also have a setting of a real place. For example, in *Romeo and Juliet* the dance takes place in very natural-looking rooms complete with curtains and furniture. Dance works can have an abstract setting with a bare stage complete with lighting that helps to set a mood rather than giving the audience a specific idea of where the dance is set. *Overdrive* is a good example of this.

> **Key terms**
>
> **Cyclorama**: a large curtain or wall, often curved, positioned at the back of the stage and usually stretched to the sides and weighted on the bottom to create as flat and even a surface as possible. Usually painted white, it can be used to create interesting lighting effects.

In-the-round

In-the-round is used by some choreographers. This performing space requires the audience to make choices about what to watch and from where. The audience can be seated on two, three or four sides of the stage. Choreographers who present dances in-the-round must ensure that dancers perform to all fronts, so that the audience always has something to see.

> **Activity**
>
> 1. Look carefully at two of the professional dance works you are studying as part of your GCSE Dance course.
>   a. Can you identify the type of performing space used in each work.
>   b. Do both works use the same type of performing space?

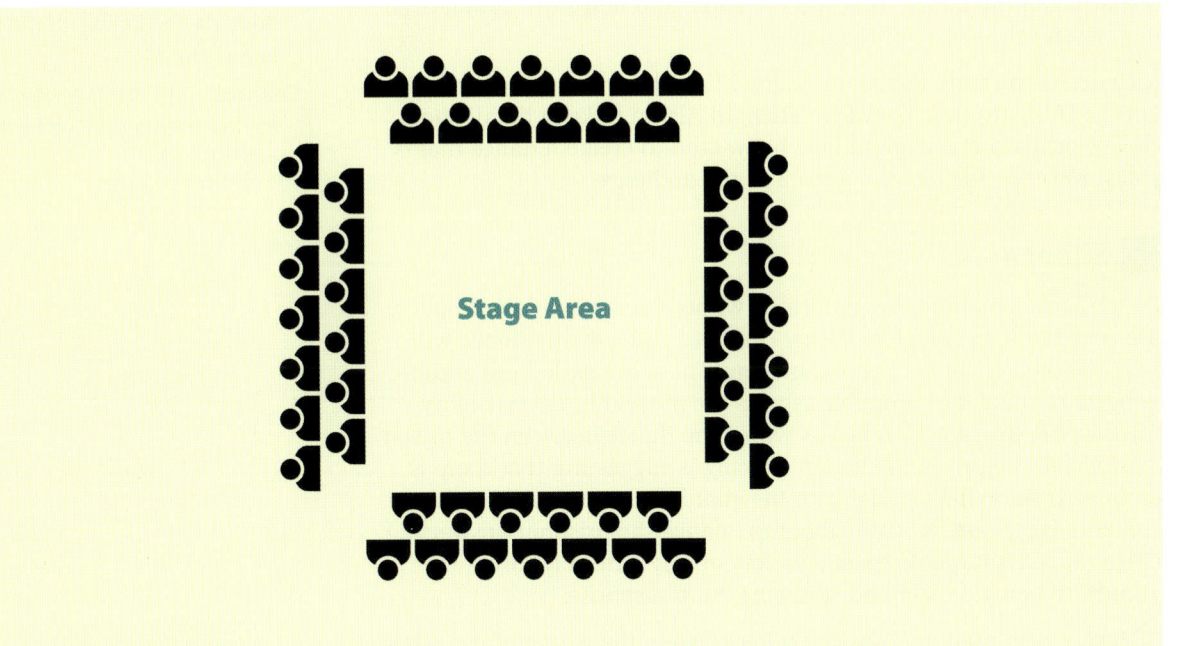

B In-the-round stage setting

Site-specific

Site-specific relates to a performance that happens in a real place (indoors or outdoors) rather than a theatre or studio, such as *Rosas Danst Rosas* which was filmed in different parts of an empty school building. Modern dance can be performed in areas other than a theatre. For example, Lea Anderson's *Cross Channel* is performed in a number of places between London and Calais, including on a train, in a hotel, on a beach and in a beach hut. *Cross Channel's* theme is a journey, and so by taking us on a real journey the audience can understand that theme more clearly.

7.4 The aural setting

Music and song

The aural setting relates to the sound used to accompany dance. This can include music, drumming, everyday or natural sound and the voice. Some choreographers use songs in their work. In *Ghost Dances*, South American folk songs are used in some sections, with dancers actually dancing to the words of the song. In works such as *Romeo and Juliet*, classical music is used to complement the style of the work – classical ballet. The music for *Romeo and Juliet*, composed by Sergei Prokofiev, helps to tell the story of the two star-crossed lovers. *'Still Life' at the Penguin Café* by David Bintley uses orchestral music, and the qualities of each animal are portrayed by the dynamics and style of the music. There is also a piece of prose read by the actor Jeremy Irons at the beginning of the dance. This sets the scene and helps the audience to understand the theme of the dance.

Richard Alston uses 'Keyboard Study #1' by Terry Riley in *Overdrive*. On the DVD, *Alston in Overdrive*, Richard Alston talks in detail about the musical score and about how he wanted to create a dance that is pleasurable for the dancers as well as the audience.

Silence

Dances can sometimes be performed without accompaniment but are very rarely in complete silence. In these cases the audience will hear the dancers breathing and moving. These are called the **audible aspects** of the dancer. Audible aspects are present in *Swansong* by Christopher Bruce, which begins with a tap dance between the prison guards and the prisoner. The tap dancing is suggesting that there is an interrogation happening, with the guards questioning the prisoner, sometimes repeatedly. Throughout the dance the prisoner answers these tapped out questions in a variety of ways: from ignoring the guards, to being defiant and stamping out a response.

Silence is also used in *Rosas Danst Rosas* when the women form a line, fall down to the floor and move in unison. The use of silence and the sound of the dancers' breathing and movement, along with repetitive and rhythmic movement, really help to build up the atmosphere and tension in this dance.

Natural sound

Natural sounds are sounds that come from nature. *Faultline*, *Bird Song* and *Perfect* use **soundscapes**. These are collections of different sounds, including the use of natural sounds such as city noises in *Faultline* and the song of the Australian Pied Butcher bird (*Bird Song*). They are used throughout to create mood or to help the audience understand the theme of the dance.

> **Objectives**
>
> Learn about different types of aural setting.
>
> Understand how different aural settings can contribute to dance works.

> **Key terms**
>
> **Audible aspects**: these are sounds that the dancers make and can include breathing, sounds of body parts tapping on the floor and slapping.
>
> **Soundscapes**: atmosphere or environments created by or with sound.

Chapter 7 Aspects of production

A *How many different sounds can you identify in this photograph that could be used in a soundscape?*

> **Activity**
>
> **1** Make a list of as many different types of aural setting as you can.
> **a** Match these to some professional dance works you have seen.
> **b** How do you think the aural setting contributes to each dance work?

■ Found sounds

Found sounds are sounds created by everyday objects that can be used to enhance the meaning of dance works. Choreographers such as Lea Anderson often use found sounds such as tannoy announcements or car horns to suggest the reality of the works she creates, as well as enhancing the minimalist style of her work.

> **AQA Examiner's tip**
>
> Choreographers choose their music with care. Think carefully about the accompaniment you choose for your solo composition task and choreography for a solo or group.

7.5 Features of accompaniment

Accompaniment is chosen for dance because of the features within it. Choreographers can use these features:

- as starting points
- to highlight specific moments in the choreography
- to enhance the idea of the theme for the choreography.

The following features could be considered when selecting accompaniment for a dance work.

> **Objectives**
>
> Learn about the different features of accompaniment.
>
> Understand how different features of accompaniment can contribute to dance works.

Style

As you discovered earlier in this book, there are many different dance styles. The same is true of music. Style can be used to describe a particular technique that has specific rhythm or sound. Styles and techniques are always changing and developing because, like choreographers, composers are influenced by the time and world in which they live. Christopher Bruce used music by the Rolling Stones when creating *Rooster* because he wanted to capture the mood of the 1960s, the decade in which he was a young man.

Tone

This means the characteristics of sound that relate to its pitch, strength or quality. Tone is a distinctive quality of sound.

Timbre

This is the character or quality of a sound that distinguishes one voice, instrument or other sound from another.

Texture

This relates to the relationships between melody, rhythm and harmony. You can hear different layers of sound in *Overdrive* by Richard Alston. These layers add texture to the sound. Alston used the idea of layers in his choreography and matched the layers of sound by layering the movement.

Rhythm

Rhythm is a repeated pattern of movements or sounds.

Pulse

Pulse is a strong, regular beat or a series of rhythmic beats. If you think about a pop song, it will usually have a very regular beat in 4/4 time. You can hear a very regular beat to the music in the ballroom scene of *Romeo and Juliet* by Kenneth MacMillan.

Pitch

Pitch relates to the frequency of a note. You can hear a very high-pitched squeak from the flea in *'Still Life' at the Penguin Café*. This is used to suggest that the flea is shocked by events happening in the dance as the morris dancers try to hit her with their sticks.

Climax

The climax is an important or exciting moment or moments in music, or a highlight. In *Ghost Dances* by Christopher Bruce you can hear the music build in intensity in each section and finally the music stops at a really dramatic moment. The movement stops at the same time, creating a climax. This tells the audience that something important has happened – a life has been taken. The climax does not need to be a building up of rhythm or volume, it could be the opposite, decreasing to silence as in *Bird Song*. Improvisation 1, immediately before the *Bird Song* central solo, and Improvisation 2, immediately after it, are performed in silence to emphasise the central solo as the most important section and indeed the starting point of the work.

Intensity

This is an extreme force, degree or amount. The rhythmic ticking sound during the section on chairs in *Rosas Danst Rosas* by Anne Teresa De Keersmaeker gradually increases in volume and speed. The movement follows this intensity, by becoming faster and more urgent. You can also hear the dancers' breathing becoming faster, which, along with the accompaniment and movement, helps to build up the tension of the dance.

Instrumentation

This relates to the arrangements of instruments that are used to perform a piece of music. You can hear traditional South American instruments such as pan pipes in Christopher Bruce's *Ghost Dances*. This use of traditional instruments helps to suggest that the work is set in South America, giving the audience a clue to the possible meaning of the work. Classical instruments such as violins are used in *Romeo and Juliet* by Kenneth MacMillan. This could suggest to the audience that this dance work is set in the past.

Activity

1. Think about the accompaniment you have selected for your choreography.
    a. Write down your reasons for choosing that accompaniment.
    b. In what ways do you think your choice of accompaniment suits your dance idea?
    c. In what ways do you think your choice of accompaniment suits the style of your dance?

7.6 The relationships between music and dance

Types of relationships

There are a variety of possible relationships between the accompaniment chosen and the movement content in dance works. Some choreographers like to work very closely with the rhythm, dynamics and sounds of a piece of music. Others use accompaniment in a more distant way, expecting the movement to stand on its own without needing accompaniment to suggest a meaning. Below are some examples of different relationships between accompaniment and movement.

> **Objectives**
>
> Learn the different relationships between accompaniment and movement.
>
> Understand how different relationships can contribute to dance works.

Close relationships

When accompaniment and movement have a close relationship, they work well together so that when the music is quiet, the dance will also be softer. When there is fast, rhythmic movement, the music is also fast and rhythmic. You can see this very clearly in works such as *Front Line* by Henri Oguike, where the movement content very closely matches the rhythm and dynamics of the music.

Sometimes the accompaniment can almost suggest an exact movement to perform. Christopher Bruce uses this relationship in several of his works. In the opening section of *Rooster*, for example, the male dancer struts with a long stride, his hands in front of him thrusting his head backwards and forwards like a rooster as The Rolling Stones sing 'I'm your little red rooster'. This adds some humour to the work and suggests that the male dancer is arrogantly strutting like a rooster.

A *Rooster, choreographed by Christopher Bruce*

During a dance performance the music you hear can help you to identify with the main characters of the dance. In the fairground scene of *Petrushka* by Michel Fokine, you know that the magician is evil as you can hear very sinister music when he appears on stage and when he enters Petrushka's room. This suggests the power that the magician has over the puppets.

Indian and African dance often use the idea of question and answer, where the dancer and the musician work in close harmony. The musician may play a rhythm for the dancer to answer or may indicate to the dancer when to change rhythm or steps.

Accompaniment and movement can happen at the same time but are not necessarily meant to work together. The music is almost like a background for the movement. You can hear this in Four Corners 1 in *Bird Song* by Siobhan Davies.

Distant relationships

When the accompaniment is created completely independently of the dance, the relationship could be described as a distant one. Merce Cunningham is a pioneer of this method. His dancers often do not hear the final accompaniment until the first time the piece is performed, and if the movement and accompaniment match at any time then this is a coincidence. This relationship supports Cunningham's idea that the movement and the sound should be able to stand separately as both have their own artistic merits.

Activities

1. Watch a section of a professional work that you are studying for your GCSE course, and pay particular attention to the music that you hear.

2. Is the relationship between the dance and accompaniment close or distant? Give reasons for your answer.

7.7 Features of costume

The costumes that a choreographer chooses for their dance work can help the dancer to get into character and the audience to make sense of the work.

Masks

The use of masks in a work can make the dance theme very clear to an audience. Masks also help to distinguish the different characters and can make the dancers look less human. In *'Still Life' at the Penguin Café* by David Bintley, most of the main characters wear either a full-face or a half-face mask. This helps the audience to recognise who the characters are. The ghost characters in *Ghost Dances* by Christopher Bruce wear skeleton masks, telling the audience that they are creepy, inhuman characters.

Length

The length of a costume can be significant. In *Romeo and Juliet* by Kenneth MacMillan, Juliet wears a short dress. This suggests that she is young. Her mother and the other adult female characters wear full-length dresses to suggest maturity.

Fabric

The choice of fabric for dancers can suggest wealth. In *Romeo and Juliet*, the use of velvet suggests that Juliet and her family are well off. Tight-fitting fabric could be chosen by a choreographer to help sculpt the body and make movement very clear to the audience. Choreographers can use costumes to suggest a period of time in which the dance work is set. The use of shiny fabric in *Faultline* suggests that the dance is set in a modern era and is dealing with current issues.

> **Objectives**
> Learn about the different features of costume.
>
> Understand how different features of costume can contribute to dance works.

> **Activity**
> 1 Think of two advantages and two disadvantages of wearing a full-face mask when dancing.

A *The denim worn by the rat in* 'Still Life' at the Penguin Café *helps to conjure up American folk style*

Colour

Colour in costumes can be used to highlight dancers, as can be seen with the neon strips on the costumes in *Bird Song*. Colour can also enhance the dance idea. For example, in *Swansong*, the khaki outfits suggest that the guards are from the military, and the prisoner's red T-shirt could suggest blood. The outfits in *Nutcracker!* change from black, white and grey to multi-coloured in the second half of the dance to show us that Clara is now in Sweetieland.

Texture

Texture can add depth and movement to a costume, helping the audience to identify characters in works. In *Ghost Dances* the ghosts' matted hair is attached to their masks, suggesting decomposing, dead characters. The liquorice allsorts in *Nutcracker!* wear shiny, rubber-effect wigs, suggesting they are made from liquorice.

Footwear

Different footwear can help to identify characters, suggest mood or build tension. It can support the style of a dance or can be used to let the audience understand the meaning of the dance. In *Romeo and Juliet*, Juliet wears pointe shoes that suit the style of the work. Pointe shoes are also worn by the flea in *'Still Life' at the Penguin Café*, and this helps the audience to understand her character as the shoes elongate her legs like a flea. In *Swansong* the dancers wear jazz shoes and tap dance the interrogation sequences. This helps the audience to understand the theme of the dance as they hear the interrogation taking place.

Activity

2. Look at the photographs on pages 16–17. Choose two photographs and describe the features of the costume. What are the similarities and differences?

B *How might these boots enhance the character or meaning in a dance?*

7.8 Dance for the camera

The effect of filming on a dance

When you see professional dance works on television or DVD you often see the dance in a totally different way to how you would see it in a theatre. In fact Lea Anderson completely reworked a dance she had already created called *Birthday* because it was being filmed for a television programme called *Tights, Camera, Action*. She named this new version *Perfect Moment*.

Filming a piece can totally change how an audience views a dance work. Choreographers often use the opportunity that filming a piece for camera presents to let the audience see specific movements or floor patterns. Using different camera techniques allows a dance work to take on a new meaning. Below are some examples of camera techniques.

Top shot

This is where there is a camera positioned above the performers, looking down on the dancers. By using top shots the choreographer can show the audience floor patterns in the work as well as how the space is used. Top shots can also show lighting or projection effects clearly if the lights are shone onto the dance floor. You can see this camera technique in Section 4a in *Bird Song* by Siobhan Davies.

> **Objectives**
> Learn about different types of camera techniques.
> Understand how different camera techniques can contribute to dance works.

> **Did you know ??????**
> Movie director and musical choreographer Busby Berkeley made the top shot popular, using it in his musicals in the 1930s. He built a platform that would hoist him up towards the roof of the film set and he shot his footage from up there.

A *Siobhan Davies' dance,* Bird Song *(2004)*

Close-up

For a close-up, the camera will zoom in very close to the dancers to focus on the dancer's leg or their facial expression, a prop and so on. This helps the audience to see in detail what is happening on the stage. You can see close-ups at the beginning of *Swansong* by Christopher Bruce, where the camera is right in the prisoner's face. This close-up shot tells the audience that the prisoner has no privacy.

Long shot

This type of shot shows a scene from a distance and gives the audience an idea of everything that is happening on a stage.

Medium shot

This shows part of the dancer's body, perhaps from the waist up or from the waist down. This type of shot can be used to show the relationship between dancers, or it can be used to focus the audience's eye on a particular movement or gesture.

Slow motion

Sometimes the dance action will be slowed down using a camera. Slow motion can be used to focus on an important moment in a dance. Mats Ek uses slow motion in *Wet Woman*, a solo in two halves. In the first half, the dancer Sylvie Guillem dances around a table, staying close to it, performing very housewife-type actions and movements such as wiping the table. In the second half she changes from performing small, closed movements (where her limbs remain close to her body) to more expansive, bigger movements that move away from the table. The use of slow motion in the middle suggests the change that she has gone through.

A camera can be used to follow the action of the dancers, helping to reinforce the dynamic qualities of the movements and the intensity of the choreography. This is used in *Rosas Danst Rosas* where the camera follows the dancers from room to room.

Film as projection

Film can be projected onto a backdrop and used in a dance work. *Faultline* begins with film of some young Asian people before the dance begins. This gives the audience an idea of the theme of the dance. *Perfect* uses images of the dancers throughout the work, suggesting the passing of time.

Activity

1. Think of a synchronised swimming routine.
   a. Choose four different camera techniques that you could use to film it successfully.
   b. What effect would your chosen camera techniques have on the finished routine?

7.9 Other people involved in dance performance

When you go to a dance performance you will naturally spend most of your time in the theatre watching the movement you see on the stage. But there are many other people, both at the front of house as well as behind the scenes, who are involved in making a public performance happen. Some of the people involved and the roles they carry out are described below.

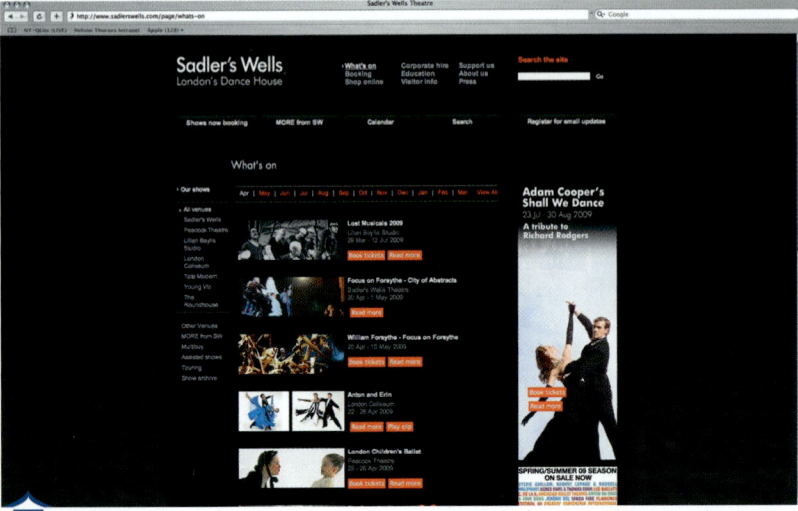

Objectives

Discover what other people are involved in a dance performance.

Understand the roles of those people.

A *Marketing departments use the internet as a way of advertising future performances*

Publicity

People who are involved in publicity are responsible for advertising and promoting dance works. They create flyers and posters, arrange for advertisements to appear in newspapers and magazines, issue press releases and send advertising material to various organisations including schools and colleges.

Marketing

The marketing manager helps with developing, monitoring and evaluating the events taking place in a theatre. They are concerned with planning to meet the goals relating to ticket sales and attendance at the theatre.

Stage manager

The stage manager is responsible for coordinating the entire stage during a production, including the lighting, sound, set, props, backstage crew and performers.

House manager

The house manager is responsible for the audience and the auditorium. It is the house manager's duty to make sure that the audience arrive and are seated on time.

Key terms

Auditorium: the place in a theatre or building where the audience sit or stand to watch a performance.

Collaboration: when choreographers, dancers and or/artists work together to create the end product.

Box office

The box-office staff take responsibility for ticket sales and help to coordinate audience seating.

Sound

The sound for dance performances could be live with an orchestra, musicians or singers and a conductor. Recorded music is also used for some performances, and the responsibility for this lies with a sound technician.

Set designer

Often choreographers work closely with designers to create specific sets for their works. The set designer will create the set and supervise the installation of it.

Lighting designer

Like the set designer, the lighting designer often works closely with a choreographer to create the effects wanted for the work.

Hair and make-up

Some choreographers want their dancers to wear their hair in a specific style or have particular make-up for a performance. In *Cats* by Gillian Lynne, each cat had his/her own individual cat-like make-up. In such cases a make-up artist would design the look needed.

Costume designer

Like the set, lighting and make-up, costume design is very important in a dance work. Costume designers have to think about using fabrics that suit the activity a dancer will do. In **collaboration** with the choreographer, they need to think about colour, shape and ease of movement.

B *The distinctive make-up of the Cape Zebra in 'Still Life' at the Penguin Café*

7.10 A comparison of dance works

Table **A** compares and contrasts three of the professional dance works specified by AQA. Each dance listed uses physical setting, aural setting and costume in a different way. The names of the set, lighting and costume designers and the composers of the accompaniment have been included because you may be asked to name them in your written exam paper.

> **Objectives**
>
> Compare the aspects of production featured in three professional works.

A A comparison of dance works

Name of work	Swansong	'Still Life' at the Penguin Café	Faultline
Choreographer	Christopher Bruce	David Bintley	Shobana Jeyasingh
Composer/ musicians	Philip Chambon	Simon Jeffes Penguin Café Orchestra	Scanner, Errollyn Wallen, Patricia Rozario
Accompaniment description	Electronic with natural (voice) and found sounds	Orchestral. The music in each section is influenced by the location of each animal	Voices are distorted and muted, they sound as if they are 'trapped' inside something. Textures and harmonies inspired by Bach cantatas and city sounds. Patricia Rozario's voice is stretched and amplified. Live voice over the top. Scratchy metallic sounds
Accompaniment contribution	Electronic crashes add to the tension. Stylised as in 'Tea for Two' – adds humour. Found sounds could suggest a bird calling in the prisoner's solo, linking the sound with the title. Other sounds could suggest prisoners crying out in another cell, the outside world, the prisoner's feelings/ emotions	Accompaniment influences the choreographic characteristics. Each animal is identified by its own music according to its location and/or character, for example the flea uses folk-style music that is lively and bouncy	'Trapped' sounds create tension. The soundtrack complements movement, light and film
Costume designer	Christopher Bruce	Hayden Griffin	Ursula Bombshell
Costume description	Prisoner: blue jeans, red T-shirt, jazz shoes. Guards: khaki shirt and trousers, jazz shoes, baseball hats ('Tea for Two')	Each species has a unique costume, for example: Cape Zebra: black-and-white striped unitard, face paint, mane of hair down his back to a tail. Flea: orange unitard with yellow and black bands, three-quarter face mask with antennae, pointe shoes.	Gender-specific. Boys: black, fitted shirt with three-quarter length sleeves; brightly coloured tie; wide-legged trousers. Girls: black, pleated, satin skirt; dark-grey metallic halter-neck top or black fitted see-through blouse with black bra. Make-up dark metallic. Hair pinned but loose

Chapter 7 Aspects of production

Costume contribution	Red T-shirt could suggest blood The guards dress identically to suggest power over the prisoner. Khaki suggests military Jazz shoes add to audible aspects of interrogation	Masks de-humanise the dancer and create character Animals are dressed differently to the other dancers to stand out Women in the zebra section are dressed in zebra print – this could suggest the zebra was killed for fashion, therefore it enhances the theme of endangered animals The flea's shiny segmented outfit makes the female dancer look more like a real flea	Boys: wearing metrosexual uniform for modern media world; slick, confident Girls: part of the gang so look confident. Hair and make-up give a youthful and street-orientated look
Set designer	Christopher Bruce	Hayden Griffin	Dick Straker
Set design description	Plain dark stage with a wooden chair Guards enter/exit from stage right	Each scene has a different backdrop, for example the flea scene has a backdrop showing brown fur, each strand of hair looks huge	A curved wall in two sections upstage. A large screen is solid and painted grey. A narrow screen is covered in grey gauze
Set design contribution	Plain stage suggests a prison cell Chair represents a weapon, shield, safe haven, shackles, prison bars, burden	In the flea scene the strands of hair look huge to make the flea appear tiny The hair suggests a skunk, the habitat of the flea	Both screens react differently to light and projection: the narrow screen can be see-through or solid
Lighting designer	David Mohr	John B Read	Lucy Carter
Lighting description	A shaft of white light forms a diagonal line from upstage left to downstage right Stark, dim general light Light from stage right when guards exit/enter	The flea scene uses bright lights with a spotlight on the flea, shadow is created by the light	Opening trio: boys framed in four squares of light that become enlarged. The back screen is lit at times with vertical strips and a bright light split into four sections on the floor At times there are vertical green neon lights
Lighting contribution	A shaft of light appears during the prisoner's solo. He focuses on it to suggest freedom/heaven/the outside world Light from stage right suggests only one entrance/exit General light on the dancers, but quite dim to suggest a harsh environment	Bright lights suggest the outdoors. The shadow creates humour as the flea plays with it during the dance	At the end, the lights restrict the space for the dancers, making them appear enclosed Bright light on the floor suggests a fault line, tying in with the theme Neon lights suggest street lights

Chapter summary

7

In this chapter you have learnt:

You have now learnt about the different features that together make a dance work and you can describe set design, lighting, costume and accompaniment in a variety of professional dance works. You will be expected to analyse and interpret these features in the dances you see throughout the course and to explain the possible reasons for a choreographer's choice.

As has been mentioned in earlier chapters, it is important that you know the difference between describing, analysing and interpreting different features of works so that you can answer questions in the exam paper accurately. Understanding the use of different features in a dance work will increase your comprehension and enjoyment of dance. Try the revision quiz to check that you have understood this chapter.

Activities

1. Choose two photographs of different professional works that appear in this book and compare and contrast the set design and costumes.
2. How do the set designs and costumes contribute to the dance idea?

Revision quiz

1. What is a proscenium stage?
2. Give three ways in which costumes help us to understand a dance work.
3. How can backdrop contribute to a dance work?
4. What does a 'close relationship between accompaniment and movement' mean?
5. What does in-the-round mean?
6. Name three camera techniques and explain how each one can enhance a dance work.
7. How can make-up create a character in a dance?
8. List as many people as you can who are involved in a dance performance.
9. What are the differences between an abstract and a realistic setting?
10. Think of two dance works with different types of accompaniment:
    - What accompaniment is used in each dance work?
    - What differences are there between the two works chosen?

A *How does the camera technique used here enhance the dance* Perfect?

8 Preparing for assessment

In this chapter you will learn about:
- how to prepare for the practical examinations
- how to prepare for the written paper.

How to prepare for your AQA GCSE Dance exam

This chapter tells you everything you need to know in order to succeed in your practical and written Dance examination.

What is in this chapter?

This is the time in your GCSE course when you begin to prepare for the final assessment in all of the practical areas and also the written examination – which requires a lot of preparation too. This chapter includes information about the written exam and the practical assessments which form part of your assessment for AQA GCSE Dance.

To help you prepare for the written exam, you will find:

- some tips for success
- some example questions
- some examples of answers to the questions, to help you gain a better understanding of what is expected of you in the written exam.

To help you prepare for the practical exams, you will find:

- some tips to help you succeed in the set dance, performance in a duo/group dance, the solo composition task and choreography for a solo or group
- information about the steps you should take to make sure that you perform at your very best
- information about what will happen on the moderation day.

8.1 The written exam

By the time you reach this stage of the course, you should have all the skills you need in preparation for your GCSE Dance exam. You will remember from Chapter 1, Introducing GCSE Dance, that Unit 1 of the GCSE Dance course (Critical appreciation of dance) is assessed by way of a written examination.

> **Objectives**
>
> Look at the format of the exam questions.
>
> Understand how to answer the exam questions accurately.

The questions you might expect

In the written paper you will be asked questions on two of the professional dance works that you have studied throughout the course. You could also be asked questions relating to the performance or choreographic work that you have completed during the course.

Tips for answering the questions

As you can see from the example exam questions on the opposite page, some of the questions will only require short answers and others will need longer, more detailed answers. It is very important to look at the number of marks that have been awarded to each question. This will give you some idea of the length of answer you are expected to give. It is important that you understand the differences between describing, analysing and interpreting a dance work because you will lose marks if you answer these questions incorrectly. You will also be expected to be able to describe actions, space, dynamics and relationships that are used in the professional works you have studied, in the set dance and in your performance in a duo/group and choreography. It is important to know that marks can be awarded for drawings or diagrams that answer questions accurately, so do not be afraid to use diagrams and stick figures to help explain your answers. The written examination paper contains between six and ten questions and the total number of marks is 50.

What you will be marked on

You will be marked on:

- your accurate description, analysis and evaluation of the aspects of production of two professional dance works
- your accurate description, analysis and evaluation of action, dynamic, spatial and relationship content of the chosen works
- your use of appropriate dance terminology
- your ability to reflect upon your own performance and choreography.

AQA Examination-style questions

Here are some example exam questions. Read them carefully and attempt to answer them.

1   (a)   Describe the accompaniment from one of the professional dance works you have studied.
Name of work: ……………………………………………………………
Name of choreographer: ……………………………………………………
Description of accompaniment:
……………………………………………………………………………………
……………………………………………………………………………………
……………………………………………………………………………………
……………………………………………………………………………………
……………………………………………………………………………………
…………………………………………………………………… *(2 marks)*

1   (b)   Explain how the accompaniment helps our understanding of the dance work.
……………………………………………………………………………………
……………………………………………………………………………………
……………………………………………………………………………………
……………………………………………………………………………………
……………………………………………………………………………………
…………………………………………………………………… *(3 marks)*

2   (a)   Name the costume designer for the work you have named in question 1(a) above.
……………………………………………………………………………………
……………………………………………………………………………………
……………………………………………………………………………………
……………………………………………………………………………………
……………………………………………………………………………………
…………………………………………………………………… *(1 mark)*

2   (b)   What contribution do the costumes make to the dance work you have named in 1(a) above?
……………………………………………………………………………………
……………………………………………………………………………………
……………………………………………………………………………………
……………………………………………………………………………………
……………………………………………………………………………………
……………………………………………………………………………………
……………………………………………………………………………………
…………………………………………………………………… *(3 marks)*

Turn the page to find a response to these tasks that would earn you a grade A.

A student response

1 (a) Describe the accompaniment from one of the professional dance works you have studied. *(2 marks)*

Name of work: Swansong

Name of choreographer: Christopher Bruce

Description of accompaniment:

The accompaniment for Swansong is electronic and is split into different sections. Each section has its own accompaniment. A voice can be heard during the 'Tea for Two' section, and found sounds can be heard during the prisoner's first solo. At the beginning of the dance there is silence and the dancers' feet can be heard tapping.

> **AQA Examiner's tip**
>
> A mark has been awarded here for describing the style of the accompaniment – electronic – and for stating that it is split into different sections. Another mark has been awarded for mentioning natural sounds and found sounds. The audible aspects of the dancers would also be awarded a mark. There are more than two marks-worth of answers here.
>
> For other professional dance works the candidate could have stated if lyrics are present, what instruments are used and if the dancers' breathing can be heard.

1(b) Explain how the accompaniment helps our understanding of the dance work. *(3 marks)*

The tapping of the feet suggests that the guards are questioning the prisoner. The found sounds during the solo could suggest that there are other prisoners crying out in different cells or they could suggest a bird calling from outside, it also helps create a tense atmosphere. The voice in 'Tea for Two' helps add to the humour of the beginning of the section.

> **AQA Examiner's tip**
>
> This question requires the candidate to explain if the music or sound tells us where the dance is set, suggests a time of day or season, and whether it builds tension in a dance to help us interpret the story-line. The candidate interprets the tap dancing as an interrogation, and makes suggestions about what the found sounds could represent.

2(a) Name the costume designer for the work you have named in question 1(a) above. *(1 mark)*

Christopher Bruce

2(b) What contribution do the costumes make to the dance work you have named in 1(a) above? *(3 marks)*

The guards are dressed in khaki trousers and shirts to suggest they are military men. Both are dressed identically to suggest authority over the prisoner. The prisoner is dressed differently from the guards and therefore stands out as a different character. He wears a red T-shirt which could suggest blood.

> **AQA Examiner's tip**
>
> Marks have been awarded here for:
> - suggesting that the guards are military soldiers and have power over the prisoner as they are both dressed the same
> - recognising that the prisoner stands out as he is dressed differently
> - suggesting that the colour of the T-shirt could represent blood.

It is a good idea to work through your answers: make a point, explain it or give an example then suggest how it helps us to understand the work. For example, in *Romeo and Juliet* by Kenneth MacMillan, the female dancers wear dresses to tell them apart from the male dancers. Juliet wears a short dress to show that she is young. Her mother and the nurse wear full-length dresses to show that they are mature women. Juliet's dress is made of rich velvet to show that she comes from a wealthy family.

> **AQA Examiner's tip**
>
> You could easily draw an example of a dancer's costume (and label it) from the work you have studied and be awarded full marks.

> **Remember**
>
> Answer the question. If it asks for description then describe – you will be asked to evaluate/interpret in other questions.

8.2 Preparing to be videoed for the set dance

The set dance is the only performance that is set by AQA. Consequently, it might be in a style that you are not confident performing. Make sure you know the set dance really well because this will help you to be confident when you perform for your exam. The set dance will be videoed by your teacher and sent to AQA to be marked by a GCSE examiner.

Objectives

Know how to prepare fully for the set dance.

Be prepared to perform the set dance with confidence.

Activity

1. Write a definition for the following performing skills:
   a. projection
   b. alignment
   c. extension
   d. timing.

A The set dance

Success in the set dance:
- Study the notes and watch the DVD for accuracy
- Be accurate with the space
- Be accurate with the dynamics
- Be accurate with the actions
- Try to perform it as a solo dance
- Correct your mistakes
- Show confidence
- Get feedback
- Think about your focus
- Try to understand the style
- Extend arms, legs and body where appropriate
- Have a sense of energy when you perform
- Tie hair back
- Take shoes/socks off
- Take jewellery off
- Know the dance from start to finish
- Practise, practise, practise

Tips for success

Learning the set dance

As you are learning the set dance try to be as accurate as possible in your use of actions, space and dynamics. You will need plenty of rehearsals to make sure that you give a polished performance. It is a good idea to watch the DVD of the set dance as you are learning it to see how it should be performed. Your teacher will also have some detailed notes that you can see and these will tell you how to perform more accurately.

Getting feedback

Your teacher and the other dance students in your class will observe you and give feedback. You could also ask to be filmed as you are learning the set dance and watch the recording for feedback. This is really important as it will help you to develop the strong areas of your performance and improve on your weaknesses.

Performing the set dance

If you make a mistake in the set dance, do not worry. It is important that you try to continue performing the rest of the dance rather than giving up. The same applies if you are dancing ahead of or behind the music. Try to listen to the rhythm and phrasing of the music. You will be marked on your level of physical and technical skill throughout the set dance, how well you commit to the performance, the quality of the movements, and health and safety when performing. If you giggle, chew gum, talk, play with your hair or adjust your clothes when you perform, you will not achieve full marks.

On the day of the set dance exam

Make sure that you get plenty of sleep the night before your exam. A good, healthy breakfast on the morning of the exam will give you the energy that you need for the rehearsal and the performance of the set dance. You will need water to keep yourself hydrated throughout the exam. Make sure that you warm up your body before dancing the set dance otherwise you could injure yourself during the exam. Your teacher will have a camera set up to film your performance and they may ask you to say your name and candidate number for recording purposes. You will then take up your starting position ready to perform the dance.

Activity

2 Ask your dance teacher or another dance student to observe you performing the set dance. Have you done the following?
   a Performed the steps and actions accurately.
   b Been accurate with your timing and use of space.
   c Extended through your body.
   d Used your focus well.
   e Performed with commitment.
   f Removed socks, shoes, jewellery and chewing-gum.
   g Performed movements safely.

8.3 Preparing for the performance and choreography assessment

What to expect

Like the set dance, you should have been preparing and rehearsing for your performance in a duo/group dance and your solo composition task/choreography for a solo or group. You and/or your dancers should now be ready to be assessed by your teacher and a moderator from AQA.

On the moderation day, the moderator will sit at a desk, your dance teacher will sit at another desk and both will watch and mark about 10 dancers perform the performance in a duo/group dance, the solo composition task and the choreography for a solo or group. It will probably feel like you are on *So You Think You Can Dance* or *The X Factor*, but try to stay calm! The moderator is visiting to award you marks, not to take them away.

Be prepared

On the day of the moderation it is very important that you arrive at the venue in plenty of time, you have your correct kit or costumes and you are warmed up and mentally ready to do your best. You will wait in a different room from the one where you will be assessed, so you can rehearse, keep warm and cue your music. You will be called when it is your turn to perform your duo/group dance or to show your choreography. How well you perform on this day will affect the final grade that you achieve. Remember, giggling, fiddling with your clothes, talking and chewing gum during a performance will mean that you will not be able to achieve the top marks, so take the assessment seriously.

You will probably feel nervous about dancing in front of a stranger, but the moderator will expect that. Remember, this is your work, you have taken a long time to prepare and rehearse it, so be proud of it and show it off to the best of your ability. For your choreography you should prepare a short programme note. This is to give the moderator and your teacher some information about your dance idea and it will help them to understand your choreography. The programme note should include:

- a title for your choreography
- the name of the music you have chosen and the artist or composer
- a brief statement about your dance starting point/stimulus.

Objectives

Be fully prepared for assessment.

Understand the importance of the moderation day.

Understand what will happen on the moderation day.

Activity

1. With a classmate, discuss how you should and should not look on the day of the exam. If you need a reminder, look at Photos **A** and **B** on page 28 in Chapter 3, Safe dance practice.

Chapter 8 Preparing for assessment

Activity

2 Ask a few members of your dance class to observe you performing. Ask for comments on the following:

a Your posture. Are you standing tall and poised like a dancer?

b Your eyes (focus) and facial expression. Both give a lot away if you are not confident.

c Your clothes. Are they appropriate for performing in the exam?

d Your starting and finishing position. Can you hold them until you are told to relax?

> **AQA Examiner's tip**
>
> Remember to hold your finishing position at the end of each performance. It gives a very polished look to your performance and makes you appear to be a professional.

A *Think and act like a professional*

Chapter summary

8

Good luck

You should now have a clear understanding of what you need to do to prepare and revise for both the practical and theoretical aspects of your GCSE Dance exam and you should have taken all of the steps necessary to give yourself the best chance of success.

Remember, your practical work will need lots of rehearsal and refining. This may mean that you will need to prepare a rehearsal schedule and you might have to do this in your own time rather than in your lesson times. You may need to ask your dancers to rehearse during break or lunchtimes, after school or in the half-term holidays. It is hard work and takes up a lot of time, but it will be worth it since there is no better feeling than going to perform when you are fully prepared and confident that you know what you are doing and your dancers know your choreography and are ready to perform it to the best of their ability.

You should also now know exactly what to expect during an assessment or moderation. You and your dancers will probably be nervous, but try to remember that your teacher and the moderator want you to do your best.

For the written paper you will need to revise all of the notes on the two professional dance works that you have studied in detail throughout the course. You will also need to remember all of the information you have learned in your practical dance sessions.

It is a good idea to watch the professional works several times during your revision sessions to keep them fresh in your mind. You could be asked questions about any of these. Remember, too, that drawings and/or diagrams used appropriately in the exam paper will be awarded marks, so do not be afraid to use them if they help to explain your knowledge and understanding.

9 Professional works fact file

Introduction

This fact file gives you information about the prescribed professional works that were available for purchase on DVD at the time of going to print. It is expected that more professional works will be added to the list as they become approved and available.

The fact file provides key information about each work so that you can compare different aspects 'at a glance'. It should also help to jog your memory when you revise. You will, of course, need to learn more detail about each dance in order to prepare for the written paper. Many dance companies provide resources for teachers and students. The addresses of the main dance companies and choreographers featured throughout this book are shown below.

Christopher Bruce
Rambert Dance Company,
94 Chiswick High Road,
London W4 1SH
Email: rdc@rambert.org.uk
www.rambert.org.uk

David Bintley
Birmingham Royal Ballet,
Birmingham Hippodrome,
Thorp Street, Birmingham B5 4AU
Email: info@brb.org.uk
www.brb.org.uk

Kenneth MacMillan
The Royal Ballet
Royal Opera House, Bow Street,
Covent Garden, London
WC2E 9DD
Email: education@roh.org.uk
www.roh.org.uk

Matthew Bourne
New Adventures,
c/o Sadler's Wells, Rosebery
Avenue, London EC1R 4TN
Email: info@new-adventures.net
www.new-adventures.net

Motionhouse Dance Theatre
Spencer Yard, Leamington Spa,
Warwickshire CV31 3SY
Email: info@motionhouse.co.uk
www.motionhouse.co.uk

Richard Alston Dance Company
Essential Alston, The Place, 17
Duke's Road, London WC1H 9PY
Email: info@theplace.org.uk
www.theplace.org.uk

Rosas and Anne Teresa de Keersmaeker
Van Volxemlaan 164,
1190 Brussels, Belgium
www.rosas.be

Shobana Jeyasingh Dance Company
Moving Arts Base, Syracusae,
134 Liverpool Road, Islington,
London N1 1LA
Email: admin@shobanajeyasingh.co.uk
www.shobanajeyasingh.co.uk

Siobhan Davies Dance Company
85 St George's Road,
London SE1 6ER
Email: info@siobhandavies.com
www.siobhandavies.com

9.1 Bird Song and Faultline

■ Bird Song

Choreographer: Siobhan Davies

Company: Siobhan Davies Dance Company

Date first performed: April 2004

Accompaniment: Andy Pink (sound score and music design)
A collage of natural and found sounds, digital samples, classical and jazz music, and silence

Costume: Genevieve Bennett
Vests and loose trousers in whites, blues and greys, with glimpses of lemon, adapt to the lighting and enhance the movement

Lighting: Adrian Plaut
Video projection is used as a light source and creates patterns and textures on the floor. Lights set above the audience illuminate the stage and the dancers.

Contributing artist: David Ward

Set/production design: Sam Collins
Patterns and effects are projected on the square dance floor.

Staging: In-the-round, later reworked for proscenium arch in 2005

Dancers: Five women and three men – Tammy Arjona, Laurent Cavanna, Gill Clarke, Henry Montes, Pari Naderi, Mariusz Raczynski, Sasha Roubicek, Sarah Warsop

Dance style: Contemporary, release based

Choreographic style: Abstract. Collaborative – dancers create their initial material and roles. Movement, sound and design closely relate

Theme: Movement responding to sound, inner rhythms, territory, signals

Starting point/inspiration: The call of the Pied Butcher bird; dance/music relationship; in-the-round performance; central solo

Structure/sections: 16 sections. Central solo choreographed first. Most of the sections 1–8 are repeated and developed in the second part, in reverse order

> **Key terms**
>
> **Release:** a dance technique using natural alignment and movement and in which breath and momentum initiate the action.

A Bird Song

Faultline

Choreographer: Shobana Jeyasingh

Company: Shobana Jeyasingh Dance Company

Date first performed: February 2007

Accompaniment: Scanner (sound artist) and Errolyn Wallen (composer)

Soprano: Patricia Rozario
Live and recorded solo voice with recorded sounds inspired by Bach and city life

Costume: Ursula Bombshell
Each is different. Urban and sophisticated. Shades of black and grey with brightly coloured ties for the men. Variety of textures in women's costumes: metallic, shiny, flimsy

Lighting: Lucy Carter
Inspired by the film and street images. Highlights tension and the urban environment. Enhances the film idea by zooming in, panning out and 'painting' the screen. Floor lights define the space and harshly light the dancers

Set: Dick Straker
A curved wall in two sections provides a surface for the film projection. One section is covered in canvas, the other in gauze – these react differently to the projection and conceal or reveal the singer. Two curved areas (one large and one narrow) are created for the dancers

Staging: Proscenium with film
Black-and-white film, shot by Pete Gomes, is projected in two sections: documentary style, young men in the street and Patricia Rozario. Techniques include rapid frame montage and superimposing

Dancers: Four women and four men

Dance style: Combines elements of Bharata Natyam and contemporary, with some pedestrian gestures

Choreographic style: Narrative and cinematic, combines the everyday with classical Indian mythology

Themes: Youth culture, gender stereotypes, gangs, city life

Starting point/inspiration: *Londonstani*, a novel by Gautam Malkhani. Peter Gomes' film. Music by Scanner

Structure/sections: Film prologue; three dance sections; film

B Faultline

9.2 Ghost Dances and Nutcracker!

Ghost Dances

Choreographer: Christopher Bruce

Company: Various, including Rambert Dance Company

Date first performed: 1981

Accompaniment: South American songs and folk tunes by Inti-Illamani and wind effects

Costume: Belinda Scarlett
Ghosts have skull-like masks and bodies painted to suggest bones and muscles. They wear wigs and rags. The Dead wear gender-specific, everyday clothes suggesting different walks of life. Each of the Dead wears a unique costume

Lighting: Nick Chelton
Gloomy and shadowy, side lighting highlights the ghosts. Brighter for folk-type dances performed by the Dead. Lighting changes signify deaths

Set: Christopher Bruce
The painted backdrop represents a rocky plain and a cave opening. In the distance there is water and mountains. There are rock-like structures on stage

Staging: Proscenium

Dancers: Five women and six men

Dance style: A blend of contemporary (Graham-influenced) and ballet with elements of folk and social styles

Choreographic style: Thematic and episodic with narrative elements. Strong characterisation

Theme: Political oppression in Chile

Starting point/inspiration: The music and South American rituals and culture

Structure/sections: Seven sections, each characterised by a different piece of music or song

A Ghost Dances

Chapter 9 Professional works fact file

■ Nutcracker!

Choreographer: Matthew Bourne

Company: First performed by Adventures in Motion Pictures

Date first performed: August 1992

Accompaniment: Pyotr Ilyich Tchaikovsky
Classical, orchestral. Composed in 1892 for the original Ivanov ballet

Costume: Anthony Ward
Colourful and 'over the top' to show characters. Cultural influences and literal references to sweets

Lighting: Howard Harrison
Theatrical, helps to create atmosphere

Set: Anthony Ward
Partly realistic but larger than life and almost cartoon-like. Scene 1 is an austere, drab orphanage with iron beds. There is an interval scene on a frozen lake and Scene 2, entered through a large mouth, represents Sweetieland – complete with a massive three-tier wedding cake

Staging: Proscenium

Scenario: Matthew Bourne and Martin Duncan

Dancers: 24 dancers

Dance style: Contemporary and balletic. Exaggerated but realistic use of gestures

Choreographic style: A reworking of a traditional ballet. Narrative and comic influenced by film and theatre. Close relationship between dance and music

Theme: The *Nutcracker* story retold with references to adolescence, escapism, fantasy and satire

Starting point/inspiration: The classical ballet and the music. Images of Victorian childhood

Structure/sections: Two acts with nine episodes

B Nutcracker!

9.3 Overdrive and Perfect

Overdrive

Choreographer: Richard Alston

Company: Richard Alston Dance Company

Date first performed: October 2003

Accompaniment: Keyboard Study #1 by Terry Riley. The pianist is Steffan Schleirmacher
Minimalist. Written for two keyboard players as if they are 'instrumental voices' and structured by computer. Phrases or fragments of melody that interact and get shorter and shorter, stopping abruptly after 21 minutes

Costume: Jeanne Spaziani
Simple and elegant costumes are gender-specific and enhance the body design and flow of the movement. Men wear grey loose-fitting vests and trousers. Women wear halter-neck tunics and trousers; three are all in red and three wear red and grey tunics and grey trousers

Lighting: Charles Balfour
The floor is washed in shades of blue, grey and purple. Colour changes relate to sections of the dance. Towards the end, spots light the floor and these elongate to create diagonals. Lighting from above and the sides creates shadows

Set: It consists of a rectangular space, with white borders at the sides and back. There are no wings. The back wall is black. Dancers exit and enter from the sides

Staging: Theatrical

Dancers: Six women and five men

Dance style: Contemporary, Cunningham influenced and release based. The torso tips, tilts, twists and curves. Movement is expansive and energetic

Choreographic style: Pure dance – concerned with the movement itself. Alston works collaboratively with the dancers to create the material. Music and dance have a close relationship – the dance interprets the music. Alston describes his approach as 'architectural', he likes structure and pattern. Use of space is multidirectional

Theme: Pattern

Starting point/inspiration: Music, movement and space

Structure/sections: 16 chapters

> **Key terms**
> **Pure dance:** a dance that is concerned with the movement itself and that has no other stimulus.
> **Multidirectional:** moving in several directions.

A Overdrive

Perfect

Choreographer: Kevin Finnan and the dancers

Company: Motionhouse

Date first performed: 2005

Accompaniment: Sophy Smith and Tim Dickinson
A mixture including percussion, voice, electric guitar. Creates atmosphere, sometimes matching and sometimes contrasting with the movement content

Costume: Claire Armitage
Simple, everyday, gender specific. Men wear white shirts and black trousers. Women wear short, strappy, black dresses

Lighting: Mark Parry
The lighting works with the film and the set. In some sections lighting divides the floor space and creates shadows. In other sections purple and gold lights achieve a bright, colourful effect

Set: Simon Dormon
Three-dimensional: a white box gradually revealing a wire cage. Many different uses. Set includes projection, sand, a paper screen, water, a gauze screen and slings. Rakes and brooms are the props

Staging: Theatrical

Other aspects of production: Film by Caroline Bridges. The *Perfect* film is by David and Mitchell Remes
Film within performance adds another layer to the choreography and meaning. Film is used to set the scene and light the dancers. Film also interacts with the dancers in the Hands section

Dancers: Three women and two men

Dance style: Combines dance theatre and aerial work. Strong physicality and contact work. Style uses and defies gravity

Choreographic style: Physically adventurous and 'filmic'. Strong emotional content. Finnan always begins with the set. Collaborative

Theme: The struggle for perfection. Time as a force that shapes us and ages us. A race against time

Starting point/inspiration: Themes of perfection and time. A book called *The History of Barbed Wire*

Structure/sections: 13 sections

B Perfect

9.4 Romeo and Juliet and Rosas Danst Rosas

Romeo and Juliet

Choreographer: Kenneth MacMillan

Company: Various, including The Royal Ballet

Date first performed: February 1965

Accompaniment: Sergei Prokofiev's Romeo and Juliet, Opus 64
Classical, orchestral

Costume: Nicholas Georgiadis
Rich and lavish. Realistic, suggesting time, place and social class (Renaissance Italy)

Lighting: Original design by William Bundy, more recently attributed to John B Read
Theatrical. Suggests time of day. Used dramatically in night-time balcony and tomb scenes. The spotlight highlights the romantic duets between the lovers

Set: Nicholas Georgiadis
Realistic. Represents various locations, indoor and outdoor. The main set is a timber-framed structure on two levels with staircases, balconies, arches and doorways. The effect is grand, old and worn. Some features are significantly over-large, for example the birdcages in Juliet's bedroom. A range of realistic props enhance characters and locations

Staging: Proscenium

Dancers: A large cast, including 14 soloists

Dance style: Ballet

Choreographic style: Narrative and dramatic. MacMillan explores behaviour and emotions in depth

Themes: Forbidden love, family conflict, growing up

Starting point/inspiration: Shakespeare's play

Structure/sections: Three Acts with 13 scenes
Other significant features: The role of Juliet was created for Lynn Seymour but the ballet is also remembered as a vehicle for the partnership of Margot Fonteyn and Rudolph Nureyev

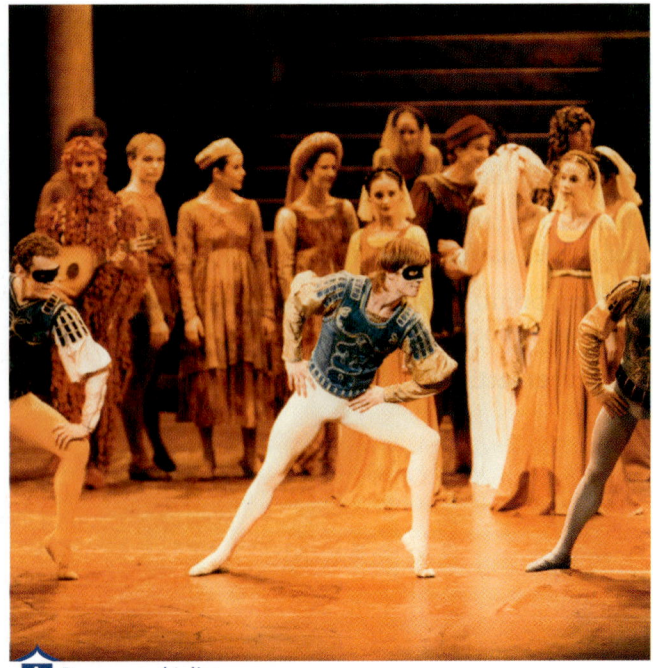

A Romeo and Juliet

Rosas Danst Rosas

Choreographer: Anne Teresa de Keersmaeker and Thierry de Mey

Company: Rosas

Date first performed: 1983. The filmed version was made in June 1996

Accompaniment: Thierry de Mey and Peter Vermeersch
Electronic, percussive, minimalist music and the natural sounds of the dancers in action

Costume: Rosas
Drab everyday grey skirts and tops, black leggings, socks and shoes. Loose-fitting and functional. They appear institutional

Lighting: Natural light through the windows

Set: The dance takes place in the corridors and rooms of a large, austere, empty school in Belgium. Windows, doors and walls frame the action. An assortment of wooden chairs is used for one section

Staging: Site specific

Other aspects of production: Film directed by Thierry de Mey. The camera becomes both composer and the choreographer by taking us on a journey, panning and zooming, selecting and layering images to create rhythms

Dancers: Four women

Dance style: Post-modern, physical with pedestrian actions and repetitive, compulsive gestures. Energetic and dynamic

Choreographic style: Highlights single parts of the body, drawing attention to small human gestures. Movements are patterned and structured to create rhythms and perfect unison is achieved

Theme: Human behaviour, rage

Starting point/inspiration: unknown

Structure/sections: Eight sections

B Rosas Danst Rosas

9.5 'Still Life' at the Penguin Café and *Swansong*

'Still Life' at the Penguin Café

Choreographer: David Bintley

Company: The Royal Ballet and Birmingham Royal Ballet

Date first performed: March 1988

Accompaniment: Simon Jeffes, Penguin Café Orchestra
Orchestral, combining classical, rock and country influences

Costume: Hayden Griffin
Combines animal and human characteristics in a dream-like way. Masks and headdresses have animal features such as curly horns and antennae. Costumes and accessories have cultural and social references

Lighting: John B Read
Lighting indicates beginnings and ends of acts. Follow-spots highlight the dancers. Colour is used to enhance the mood, bright in the first half and dramatic towards the end

Set: Hayden Griffin
Set in a café with chairs and tables. After the opening scene the rest of the dances take place on bare stage. Props include waiters' trays. Ever-changing colourful backdrops give a sense of environment, climate and scale

Staging: Proscenium

Dancers: Nine soloists plus corps de ballet

Dance style: Modern ballet with a mix of social and cultural styles to suggest geographical locations. These include English morris, Latin American carnival and African dance styles. There are also references to contemporary and post-modern dance

Choreographic style: Episodic. Combines a range of styles and cultural influences to tackle a political theme. Theatrical, using characterisation and humour to good effect

Theme: Endangered species

Starting point/inspiration: The music and the album cover. *The Doomsday Book of Animals* by David Day

Structure/sections: Introduction followed by eight scenes

A 'Still Life' at the Penguin Café

Swansong

Choreographer: Christopher Bruce

Company: Various, including Rambert Dance Company

Date first performed: November 1987

Accompaniment: Philip Chambon
Electro-acoustic with digitally sampled sounds, vocals, a reed pipe and popular dance rhythms. Unaccompanied interludes enable us to hear the tapping of feet. Composed in collaboration with the choreographer

Costume: Christopher Bruce
Everyday clothes associated with roles. Uniforms for the interrogators and jeans and T-shirt for the victim.

Lighting: David Mohr
Overhead lighting and a diagonal shaft of light to suggest natural light from upstage left. Footlights create shadows. Atmospheric

Set: Christopher Bruce
Bare stage except for a chair, suggests a cell. Interrogators always exit stage right (a door?). The chair has many purposes and is used symbolically as a weapon, a shield and shackles. Props (canes and a red nose) are used to degrade the victim

Staging: Proscenium

Dancers: Three men (also performed by three women, and a mixed cast)

Dance style: Contemporary, with physical contact and some balletic movements. Includes references to social and theatrical dance

Choreographic style: Episodic, dramatic, thematic

Theme: Human rights; prisoner of conscience

Starting point/inspiration: The work of Amnesty International; saying goodbye (to a career as a dancer); the experiences of Chilean poet Victor Jara and the novel, *A Man*, by Oriana Fallaci

Structure/sections: Introduction followed by seven sections. The victim remains on stage throughout and performs a solo in section 3 which has motifs that are repeated and/or developed in sections 5 and 7

B Swansong

More dance companies

Akram Khan Dance Company
www.akramkhancompany.net

CandoCo Dance Company
www.candoco.co.uk

The Cholmondeleys and Featherstonehaughs
www.thecholmondeleys.org

English National Ballet
www.ballet.org.uk

Henri Oguike Dance Company
www.henrioguikedance.co.uk

Jasmin Vardimon Dance Company
www.jasminvardimon.com

Jonzi D Productions
www.jonzi-d.co.uk

Ludus Dance
www.ludusdance.org

Northern Ballet Theatre
www.northernballettheatre.co.uk

Phoenix Dance Theatre
www.phoenixdancetheatre.co.uk

Union Dance
www.uniondance.co.uk

Dance information and resources

Akādemi (South Asian Dance in the UK)
For South Asian dance resources
www.akademi.co.uk

Arts Pool Interactive guides to *Birdsong*, *Faultline*, *Perfect* and *Swansong*. Guides to other prescribed works to follow.
www.arts-pool.co.uk

CDET (Council for Dance Education and Training)
For information about dance training and careers
www.cdet.org.uk

CICD (Centre for Indian Classical Dance)
For classical Indian dance resources
www.cicd.org.uk

Dance Books
For books, DVDs and music
www.dancebooks.co.uk

Dance UK
For information about safe dance practice
www.danceuk.org

English Folk Dance and Song Society
For books, music and information about English folk dance
www.efdss.org

Freeplay music
For downloading music for educational purposes
www.freeplaymusic.com

Laban
For courses, books, archive material, videos and DVDs
www.laban.org

National Resource Centre for Dance
For resource packs, DVDs, videos, courses and archive material
www.surrey.ac.uk/NRCD

Youth Dance England
For information about dance careers, resources, youth dance events and opportunities
www.yde.org.uk

Websites for teachers

AQA
www.aqa.org.uk

National Dance Teachers Association
www.ndta.org.uk

Glossary

A

Abstract actions or features that denote the quality or essence of the original.

Accents placement of stress on a beat or a movement.

Accessory an additional item of costume, for example gloves.

Accompaniment the sound that you hear during the dance, for example percussion.

Accumulation when a dancer begins a series of movements and others join in until they all dance in unison.

Actions what a dancer does, for example leap, spin, balance.

Aesthetic something we judge to be appealing and tasteful.

Alignment the correct placement of body parts in relation to other body parts.

Analyse examine and explain a dance work in detail.

Appreciate show knowledge and understanding of your own and others' dances and of dance in general.

Asymmetric uneven.

Audible aspects these are sounds that the dancers make and can include breathing, sounds of body parts tapping on the floor and slapping.

Auditorium the place in a theatre or building where the audience sit or stand to watch a performance.

Aural setting audible accompaniment to the dance such as music, words, song, soundscape, etc.

B

Backdrops walls or drapes at the back of the stage usually painted with a decorative scene, picture or design.

Balance a steady or 'held' position.

Bharata Natyam a classical South Asian dance style, characterised by intricate hand gestures and fast footwork.

Binary a composition in two sections.

C

Canon when movements overlap in time.

Chance a method of choreography in which dance material is determined or manipulated using a random method, for example by throwing dice.

Character/isation a role or part expressed by a dancer.

Choreographic approaches how choreographers work with the dance material, for example by using the dancers' improvisations.

Choreographic devices using different methods to repeat, develop and vary the material.

Choreographic form giving the dance a shape and structure, for example by using contrasting sections.

Choreography the art of creating dance.

Climax the most important or significant moment of the dance, which usually happens near the end.

Collaboration when choreographers, dancers and or/artists work together to create the end product.

Complementary actions or shapes that are similar but not exactly the same.

Composition a dance.

Contact when dancers touch, lean, lift or support each other.

Contact improvisation work is created through weight-taking etc.

Contemporary a group of dance styles originating in the early 20th century created individuals working outside the Classical ballet style, in response to the conditions of modern life.

Contraction shortening of a muscle or muscles.

Contrasting shapes or movements which are very different from each other.

Core stability relates to the use of the centre to stabilise the body during movement.

Counterpoint when two or more dancers perform different phrases at the same time.

Cyclic something which has a circular feeling and which ultimately comes back to its own beginning.

Cyclorama a large curtain or wall, often curved, positioned at the back of the stage and usually stretched to the sides and weighted on the bottom to create as flat and even a surface as possible. Usually painted white, it can be used to create interesting lighting effects.

D

Describe write or talk about what something looks or sounds like or is made up of.

Direction the pathway of a movement.

Dynamic stretches slow, controlled movements through the full range of motion.

Dynamic variation variety in the quality or the 'how' of the movement, for example the use of different kinds of speed, energy and flow in a dance.

Dynamics the 'how' or 'quality' of movement.

E

Elevation the action of 'going up' without support, such as in a jump.

Ensemble a group of dancers performing together.

Episodic a choreography with several separate sections linked by a theme.

Evaluate to consider the value, quality or importance of something.

Extension lengthening one or more muscles or limbs.

F

Flexibility the range of movement that is attainable in a joint or muscle.

Focus using the eyes to enhance performance or interpretative qualities.

Formations shapes or patterns created by a group of dancers.

Fugue interwoven phrases of movement or music.

G

Gestures actions or movements of a body part that is not weight bearing.

Graham-based a contemporary dance style created by Martha Graham in the 1930s. Characterised by angular body shapes and use of breath and the centre of the body to initiate movements.

H

Highlights moments in the dance that draw attention to or emphasise something important.

Hydrated provided with an adequate amount of water.

I

Improvise to explore and create movements without planning.

Interpret understand and explain the meaning of a dance through action, costume, set design/lighting and accompaniment.

In-the-round a performing area with the audience seated on all sides.

Isolation moving a part of the body independently, such as a shoulder shrug.

K

Krumping a competitive, freestyle form of street dance in which dancers interact.

L

Lactic acid a waste product which builds up in the muscles during exercise.

Level distance from the ground, for example low, medium or high.

Literal actions or features that closely represent the subject, theme or idea.

M

Motifs patterns or designs of action content that encapsulate an idea and can be repeated and developed throughout the dance.

Multidirectional moving in several directions.

Musicality the ability to pick out the unique qualities of the accompaniment and make them evident through the performance.

N

Narrative a dance that tells a story.

Numerical variation how the number of dancers in a group is used.

Nutrition obtaining the food necessary for health.

P

Perform prepare and dance a piece to an audience.

Peripheral vision what you can see happening at the outer edges of your range of vision without actually moving your eyes or your head.

Phrase a sequence of linked movements.

Posture body position.

Projection when a dancer gives out appropriate energy to connect with an audience and draw them into the performance.

Props portable objects that are used in a dance for example a suitcase or newspaper.

Proscenium the arch or opening which separates a stage from the auditorium.

Pure dance a dance that is concerned with the movement itself and that has no other stimulus.

R

Relationships the 'with what or whom' of movement. How dancers dance together.

Release a dance technique using natural alignment and movement and in which breath and momentum initiate the action.

Repetition performing the same action or phrase again.

Rhythm repeated patterns of movements or sounds.

Risk assessment identification and assessment of potentially harmful factors.

Rondo a musical form with an alternating and repeated section.

S

Site-specific dances that are designed for non-theatre spaces, for example for a museum, the beach, etc.

Soundscapes atmosphere or environments created by or with sound.

Space the 'where' of movement.

Style characteristic features of a dance work or choreographer's work that enable it to be recognised as belonging to that particular group.

Symbolic actions or features that suggest or convey an idea, theme or feeling, for example the thumbs up gesture.

Symmetric the same on both sides or an equal balance of parts.

Syncopated stressing a beat that is not normally stressed.

T

Technical skill the ability to control what the body does.

Technique a specific way of moving according to particular rules and conventions.

Ternary a composition in three sections, that is, A B A.

Theme and variation where each section of a composition develops from the one before.

Transitions links between dance phrases or sections.

Index

Headings and page numbers in **bold** type indicate Key Terms.

A

abstract **44**, 51, 88
accents **38**
accessory **67**
accompaniment **9**, 92–3, 94–5
  see also music
accumulation **56**
actions **12**, 34–5
aesthetic **28**
African dance 11, 12
Akādemi 126
Akram Khan Dance Company 126
Alston, Richard 16, 58, 90, 92, 115, 120
analyse **5**
Anderson, Lea 89, 91, 98
appreciate **7**
art 44, 47, 48
Arts Pool 126
assessment 7
  dance styles 18–19
  duo/group dance 76–7, 112–13
  preparation 105–14
  solo set dance 78, 110–11
  solo/group choreography 66–7
  written exam 106–9
asymmetric **58**, 59
audible aspects **90**
audience reaction 51
auditorium **100**
aural setting **43**, 65, 81, 90–1

B

backdrops **82**, 88, 99
balance **34**
ballet 12, 55
beginnings 53
behind-the-scenes staff 100–1
Berkeley, Busby 98
Bharata Natyam **12**, 13
Billy Elliot 5
binary **60**, 61
Bintley, David 7, 15, 17, 61, 90, 96, 102–3, 115, 124
Bird Song 48, 53, 84, 93, 98, 116
Birmingham Royal Ballet 115
body design 12
Bourne, Matthew 15, 45, 57, 84, 86, 87, 115, 119
box office 101
Bruce, Christopher 15, 17, 35, 37, 40, 52, 55, 56, 58, 61, 85, 87, 88, 92, 93, 94, 96, 99, 102–3, 115, 118, 125

C

camera techniques 81, 98–9
CandoCo Dance Company 126
canon **55**
Cats 101
CDET (Council for Dance Education and Training) 126
Centre for Indian Classical Dance (CICD) 126
chance **50**
character **44**
The Cholmondeleys and Featherstonehaughs 126
choreographic approaches **15**, 50–1
choreographic devices **15**, 52–3
choreographic form **15**
choreography **5**, 6–7, 43–68
  process 62
  solo/group 19, 59, 66–7, 112–13
  styles 9, 14–17
CICD (Centre for Indian Classical Dance) 126
classical music 90
climax **46**, 53, 93
close-ups 99
clothing 28–9
collaboration **100**, 101
collage 50–1

colour 86, 88, 97
companies 115, 126
complementary **55**
composition **48**
contact **12**, 56, 57
contact improvisation **50**
contemporary **9**, 12, 14
contraction **12**
contrasting **52**, 55
cool-down 25
copyright law 65
core stability **25**
costume 81, 85, 96–7, 101
costume designers 101
Council for Dance Education and Training (CDET) 126
counterpoint **56**, 57
creativity see **choreography**
criticism 5
Cross Channel 89
Cunningham, Merce 50, 95
cyclic **60**, 61
cyclorama **88**

D

dance companies 115, 126
dance language 12
dance planners 46–7
Dance UK 126
dance works 102–3, 116–25
dancing for the camera 81, 98–9
Davies, Siobhan 14, 45, 53, 84, 98, 115, 116
decoration of sets 86
describe **7**
designers
  costumes 101
  lighting 101
  sets 86, 101
diet 22–3
directing 5
direction **25**
Dormon, Simon 86

Index

D
downstage 36, 37
duo/group dance 59, 76–7, 112–13
dynamic stretches 25
dynamic variation 65
dynamics 12, 38–9

E
Ek, Mats 99
elevation 26
endings 53
English Folk Dance and Song Society 126
English National Ballet 126
ensemble 58
episodic 60, 61
evaluate 7, 63
examination see assessment
expression 6
expressive skills 72–3
extension 12

F
fabric (costumes) 96
fact file 115–26
Faultline 15, 57, 84, 102–3, 117
Featherstonehaughs (and Cholmondeleys) 126
feedback 111
film 98, 99
Finnan, Kevin 16, 51, 82, 86, 121
flexibility 6, 25
floor-work 12
focus 6, 72
Fokine, Michel 95
folk dance 10, 58, 126
folk songs 90
footwear 97
foreground/background 57
formations 10
found sounds 91
freeplay music 126
Front Line 45, 55, 56, 94
front-of-house staff 100–1
fugue 60, 61

G
gestures 12, 13, 34, 45
Ghost Dances 35, 37, 48, 52, 56, 58, 83, 87, 88, 93, 96, 97, 118
glossary 127–9
Graham-based 12
graphic scores 53
group choreography 19, 59, 66–7, 112–13
group dance 26, 40, 48, 59, 67, 76–7
group designs 58–9
Guillem, Sylvie 99

H
hair/make-up 101
hand gestures 13
Henri Oguike Dance Company 126
highlights 52
house managers 100
hydrated 22, 23

I
improving performance 79, 111
improvise 50, 63
in-the-round 81, 89
Indian Classical Dance (Centre) 126
information and resources 126
ingredients of dance 33–42
injuries 21, 27
instrumentation 93
intensity (sound) 93
internet 100
interpret 7
isolation 9

J
Jasmin Vardimon Dance Company 126
jazz dance 9, 12
Jeyasingh, Shobana 15, 102–3, 115, 117
joint mobility 25
Jonzi D 44, 126
jumps 21, 26, 34

K
Kanindsky, Wassily 47
Keersmaeker, Anne Teresa de 52, 54, 93, 115, 123
Kelly, Gene 45
krumping 9

L
Laban 126
lactic acid 22, 23
Lambert, Gary 44
language of dance 12
level 36, 87
lifts 26, 27
lighting 83–4, 101
lighting designers 101
literal 50, 51
long shots 99
Longevity 44
Ludus Dance 126
Lynne, Gillian 101

M
MacMillan, Kenneth 82, 93, 96, 115, 122
make-up 101
Maliphant, Russell 83
Mancini, Henry 61
marketing 100
masks 7, 96
medium shots 99
mental rehearsal 74
Mey, Thierry de 123
Miró, Joan 44, 48
mirror image 55
mirrors 39
moderation day 112
motifs 19, 48–9, 55
Motionhouse Dance Theatre 51, 82, 86, 115
movement types 51
multidirectional 120
music 45, 60, 64–5, 90, 92, 93, 94–5, 126
musicality 72

N

narrative 15, 61
National Dance Teachers Association 126
National Resource Centre for Dance 126
natural world 45, 58, 90
New Adventures 115
Northern Ballet Theatre 126
numerical variation 58
Nutcracker! 8, 57, 84, 86, 87, 97, 119
nutrition 22–3

O

Oguike, Henri 45, 55, 56, 83, 94, 126
orchestral music 90
outcomes (audience reaction) 51
Overdrive 16, 58, 90, 92, 120

P

paintings 44, 47, 48
Perfect 16, 51, 82, 86, 121
perform 5, 6
performance 69–80
  in a dance 18
  group dance 18, 26, 40, 48, 59, 67, 76–7
  safe practice 26–7
  set dance 18, 110–11
  spaces 88–9
peripheral vision 26
personal style 19–20
Petrushka 95
Phoenix Dance Theatre 126
photographs 44, 71
phrase 48
phrasing 38
physical setting 81, 82–7
physical theatre 9
The Pink Panther 61
pitch 93
planning 46–7, 74–5
posture 6
practise 74

preparation
  for assessment 105–14
  choreography assessment 112–13
  duo/group dance 112–13
  set dance 110–11
process of choreography 62
production 81–104, 116–25
professional productions 102–3, 116–25
projected images 84, 99
projection 6, 72
props 40, 45, 81, 84–5
proscenium 81, 88
publicity 100
pulse 92
pulse-raising activity 25
pure dance 120

Q

question and answer 57, 95

R

Rambert Dance Company 115
rehearsal
  clothing 28–9
  dance spaces 30–1
  effectiveness 74–5
relationships 6, 40–1, 54–7
release 116
repetition 52
resources 126
Rest, Ice, Compression, Elevation, Diagnosis (RICED) 27
rhythm 6, 92, 94, 95
RICED (Rest, Ice, Compression, Elevation, Diagnosis) 27
Richard Alston Dance Company 115
risk assessment 28, 29, 31
Romeo and Juliet 82, 88, 90, 93, 96, 122
rondo 60, 61
Rooster 92, 94
Rosas Danst Rosas 52, 54, 89, 90, 93, 123
The Royal Ballet 115

Rozario, Patricia 84

S

safe practice 21–32
set dance 18, 110–11
set design 82, 86, 101
set designers 86, 101
shape of sets 86
Shift 83
Shobana Jeyasingh Dance Company 115
silence 90
Singin' in the Rain 45
Siobhan Davies Dance Company 115
site-specific 81, 89
slow motion 99
social dance 11
solo set dance 18, 78–9
solo/group choreography 19, 59, 66–7, 112–13
songs 90
sound intensity 93
sound technicians 101
soundscapes 90
South Asian style 12, 13
space 12, 36–7
spaces for rehearsal 30–1
stage managers 100
stage space 36, 88–9
'Still Life' at the Penguin Café 7, 15, 17, 58, 61, 82, 90, 93, 96, 97, 102–3, 124
stillness 34
stimuli 44–7, 67
street dance 9, 11, 12
structure 60–1
studios 30
style 9–20, 72, 92
success tips 106, 109, 110–11, 113
supports 26
Swan Lake 45
Swansong 15, 17, 40, 55, 83, 85, 90, 97, 99, 102–3, 125
symbolic 50, 51
symmetric 58, 59
syncopated 12

T

Tag 44
tap dancing 90
Teachers Association 126
technical skills 70–1
technique 9
ternary **60**, 61
texture 86, 92, 97
theatre staff 100–1
theme and variation **60**, 61
themes 35, 89
timbre 92
tips for success 106, 109, 110–11, 113
tone (sound) 92
top shots 98
traditional dance 10
transitions **52**
travelling 34
turns 34

U

Union Dance 126
unison 54
upstage 36, 37
urban dance 9, 11, 12

V

videoed dance 110–11
visualisation 74

W

warm-up 24–5
water 23
websites 115, 126
weight sharing 26
Wet Woman 99
working with others 26, 100, 101
written exam 106–9
Wyoming 45

Y

Youth Dance England 126

Acknowledgements

The authors and publisher are grateful to the following for permission to reproduce photographs and other copyright material in this book.

Text acknowledgements

2.3 Quotation from the DVD *Alston in Overdrive* (2003) by permission of Richard Alston and The Place; Extract taken from Motionhouse Dance Theatre Student Pack by permission of the Motionhouse Dance Theatre; Extract from *'Still Life' at the Penguin Café* study pack by permission of Birmingham Royal Ballet; Extract from Jane Pritchard, Swansong Study Notes (1998) by permission of Rambert Dance Company.

Photo acknowledgements

Alamy Andrew H Williams/2.2A; Dennis Hallinan/5.1A, Martin Shields/5.7A; **Anthony Crickmay** 2.3E, 5.6B, 7.1B, 9.2B, 9.5B; **Birmingham Hippodrome** i7a; **Birmingham Royal Ballet** 2.3D, 7.7A, 9.5A; **Bill Cooper** 7.1A, 9.4A; **Brian Slater** I1A, 1.1A. I3A, 3.2A, 3.3A, 3.3B, 3.3C, 3.6A, I4A, I6A, 6.1B, 6.2B, 6.3B, 6.4A, I8A; **Bridgeman** 5.2C; **Chris Nash** 2.3C, 7.11A, 9.1B, 9.3B; **Food Standards Agency** 3.1A; **Fotolia**; Earl Robbins/2.1E; Rosemary Robenn 3.5A; **Gautier Deblonde** 2.3A; **Getty** 2.1B, Sean Murphy/2.1C; Michael Blann/2.1D, Digital Vision/2.4A; **Herman Sorgeloos**; 4.4B; 5.6A, 9.4B; **iStockphoto** Paula Connolly/2.1A, Doram 3.1B; Vicki Reid/3.4C, 7.7B, 7.7C; **Kobal Collection** 5.1B; **Lebrecht Music & Arts** Dee Conway/1.2a; **Liz Dale** 3.4A, 3.4B, 3.4D; **Maggie Clunie**; 4.1A, 8.3A; **Rambert Dance Company** 7.6A, 9.2A; **Sadler's Wells Theatre** 7.1C, 7.2A; **siobhandavies.com** 7.8A, 9.1A; **The Place** 2.3B, 9.3A; **Tom Dale** 7.3A, 7.3B, 7.4A with thanks to Bishopshalt School, Hillingdon.

Every effort has been made to contact the copyright holders and we apologise if any have been overlooked. Should copyright have been unwittingly infringed in this book, the owners should contact the publishers, who will make corrections at reprint.